The Winner's Edge

The Winner's Edge

THE CRITICAL ATTITUDE OF SUCCESS

Dr. Denis Waitley

NYT
Times
BOOKS

Published by TIMES BOOKS, a division of Quadrangle/
The New York Times Book Co., Inc., Three Park Avenue,
New York, N.Y. 10016

Published simultaneously in Canada by Fitzhenry & Whiteside,
Ltd., Toronto

Library of Congress Cataloging in Publication Data

Waitley, Denis.
The winner's edge.

Bibliography: p. 181
1. Success. I. Title.
BF637.S8W28   1980   158'.1   79–5392
ISBN 0–8129–0897–X

Manufactured in the United States of America

To my parents, Edwin and Irene,
who made me feel special.

To my wife, Susan,
who makes every day our "homecoming" celebration.

To my children, Debbie, Dayna, Denis, Darren, Kim, and
Lisa,
who give me joy today and optimism for tomorrow.

CONTENTS

The Winner's Edge

INTRODUCTION: WINNING LIVES

I grew up during the post-Depression and World War II years in San Diego, California. Like everybody else, I recall cutting pieces of cardboard and slipping them inside my shoes each morning so I wouldn't wear holes through my socks at school. We didn't have much money, but we never went to bed hungry and what clothes we had were clean. My Mom and Dad argued a lot when I was young, probably with financial pressures the underlying theme. And although they were obviously unhappy, they gave me the greatest gifts I've ever received: *early feelings of being special.*

I really first became aware that I might be worthwhile at about age nine. My Mom read me adventure stories and poetry and told me our ancestors were very creative. My Dad always relished my smallest accomplishments in school and sports and painstakingly made a ritual out of measuring my one-sixteenth-of-an-inch growth in height with a ruler and pencil on my closet door. I was a peewee for my age, but he promised me I'd be tall. (He's 5 feet and 8 inches, and I finally reached my goal of 6 feet.)

3

THE WINNER'S EDGE

My Dad gave me what I believe are the most important time frames between a parent and child: He sat on my bed each night for 5 to 10 minutes for a couple of years and told me he loved me. "I'm proud to wear your name, my son," he glowed. "I missed my ship, but you'll catch yours. You were born to win, son!" And each night, after telling me I was made of "the right stuff," he'd turn out the light in my bedroom and whisper the same thing night after night: "Remember, son, when I turn out the light for you, it goes out all over the world. Your light is the only light that shines, because life only exists through your eyes. Life is the movie you see through your own, unique eyes. It makes little difference what's happening out there, it's how *you* take it that counts."

And then he went away one night. My mother and he had had a fight. He turned out my light and, instead of his usual "Good night," said "Good-bye."

During the next several years, while my parents were separated, my mother and grandmother were the strong motivators in my life. My grandmother, who lived eighty-six beautiful years without a complaint, told me I was special. My mother challenged me to step into my father's shoes. After he went away, I learned that he was serving aboard ship in the South Pacific during the final struggles of World War II. I read and reread his once-a-month letters encouraging me to strive for excellence. My mother helped me campaign for student offices in school and gave me more responsibilities each week to help manage the household.

I began to excel. Firstly, my father expected the best from me. Secondly, my mother challenged me to get busy and put my optimism to the test. And thirdly, my parents were un-

4

INTRODUCTION

happy and unfulfilled, and I chose to be happy and fulfilled. Therein was spawned my philosophy of life: "Expect the best; convert problems into opportunities; be dissatisfied with the status quo; focus on where you want to go, instead of where you're coming from; and, most importantly, decide to be happy, knowing it's an attitude, a habit gained from daily practice, and not a result or payoff."

I was a straight "A" student throughout high school, student body president, multisport varsity letterman, graduating with honors and with a scholarship to Stanford University and an appointment to the U. S. Naval Academy at Annapolis. I went Navy and soon learned one of the greatest lessons of my life: as a Plebe during my freshman year at the Academy, I was lower on Tecumseh's totem pole than the Admiral's dog! There were thirty-seven hundred other guys at Annapolis and most of them outranked me, outran me, outscored me, outscholared me, and outshone me. I learned the wisdom of not comparing myself so much to others and began to set internal standards of excellence. I didn't like the military routine and the idea of a pecking order based upon a combination feudal system and time-in-rank. It would have been too easy to quit and high-tail it back to Stanford and the University of Southern California (USC). But my Dad had offered me some good advice before I took the Midshipman's oath: "When you hit a sour note, finish the song before you start another." And so, I stuck it out for four years and was graduated in June of 1955. It was one of the best decisions of my life.

Pensacola and Naval Aviation made my spirits soar. I felt like Jonathan Livingston Seagull. Flight training was tough, high-risk, an individual "high"—and designed for optimists only! As a carrier-based attack pilot, I came to understand the need for pinpointing targets and destinations (GOAL-SETTING). I learned that there is an almost automatic winning response or reflex developed through simulation and training (SELF-DISCIPLINE). And I tasted the essence of courage (FAITH and COMMITMENT). Flying in close formation at supersonic speeds taught me the value of interdependency and cooperation (TEAMWORK), despite the dry mouth, heart-in-throat feeling, and white knuckles.

My actual research on high-performance winning behavior began during the period 1958–1960, while I was flying a desk as a special project officer for the Navy Department at the Pentagon. As a thesis for graduate night school in semantics and propaganda, I conducted an in-depth study of Communist interrogation methods and behavior-modification techniques during the Korean War. Having become fascinated with the difference between purposeful and purposeless individuals, I left the Navy and entered the decade of the 1960's determined to find some common denominators for high achievement under stress. As a consultant to industry, I devoted four years to industrial psychology, counselling chief executives on public, market, and shareholder attitudes. I commuted weekly between Los Angeles and Wall Street studying attitudes as they related to the "bottom line."

THE TURNING POINT

The turning point in my career came in 1965, when I joined the Salk Institute for Biological Studies in my home

INTRODUCTION

town of La Jolla, California. Although my capacity at the Institute was nonscientific, I had a unique opportunity to observe that in order to approach a solution for a particular disease, the investigator must first learn how the healthy organism functions. Instead of focusing on the disease and cure, the scientist looks at life and health. To cure cancer, we need to learn how the healthy cell reproduces itself and what turns its growth on and off.

Likewise, to be a winner in life, we need to understand the critical elements of a successful attitude, not more details about losers so we can find a cure for them.

My modest contribution to the Salk Institute was to interpret the biological studies to the general public and gain financial sponsorship. I developed the Andy Williams–San Diego Open Golf Tournament, and other celebrity special events and gifts, as a means for perpetuating development capital. My reward was a glimpse into some of the finest scientific minds in the world assembled as fellows and staff members of the Institute, including the late Jacob Bronowski, who wrote the classic *The Ascent of Man,* and international Nobel laureates such as Renatto Dulbecco, David Baltimore, and Leslie Orgel.

Dr. Jonas Salk is the most brilliant, sensitive individual I have ever been privileged enough to call a friend. His counsel during critical, career-decision years, his insistence upon integrity and truth in every transaction, and his willingness to listen to inputs from a variety of intellectual levels and sources have earned my deepest respect and, outside of my immediate family, have had the most profound effects upon my life. It is because of his example that I continued my formal education for a doctorate in human behavior and later developed important contacts with many leaders in the health sciences.

During the late sixties I attended seminars and studied the works of those individuals I felt were at the cutting edge of behavioral research. I plunged into Maslow, Jung, Adler, and James. I attended lectures taught by Viktor Frankl, Herb Otto, Carl Rodgers, William Glasser, Margaret Mead, S. I. Hayakawa, and James Newman.

In early 1969, while writing a book on the Department of Defense and the Pentagon, I was commissioned to conduct a study of simulation techniques of the National Aeronautics and Space Administration (NASA) astronauts. At Houston, Texas, Granby, Colorado, and at Cape Kennedy, I observed and interviewed the crews. My favorites were Wally Schirra, Gene Cernan, Scott Carpenter (Navy pilots and great human beings), and Bill Anders (who was my classmate at the Naval Academy). I tried to relate the simulation of an Apollo moon mission to visualization practices in sports, business, and life in general. It struck me that here were grown men playing "let's pretend we're going to the moon," something that no one had ever done before and that only Jules Verne, Ray Bradbury, and Isaac Asimov had really dreamed possible. And through the application of creative imagination, team-work, and incredible, relentless simulation a pipedream became a reality!

During the early 1970's I studied the coaching and personal philosophies of John McKay, head football coach at USC; Johnny Wooden, head basketball coach at UCLA; and Don Shula, head coach of the Miami Dolphins. Each man is a fine motivator and speaker and each has a way of earning the devotion of his players without using intimidation and fear. I also sought out and became a disciple of the late Dr. Maxwell Maltz, whose longtime best seller *Psycho-Cybernetics* is, in my opinion, a premier, nontechnical book on self-image psychology.

In 1974, I became a rehabilitation volunteer for returning Vietnam veterans. My special interest was in learning about the interrogation methods used by the Viet Cong and North Vietnamese, comparing these with those of the Chinese and North Koreans, and studying the simulation experiences of our prisoners of war while they were imprisoned. These were compared with experiences of athletes, astronauts, executives, and prisoners of other wars. I was becoming convinced that survival and success were largely dependent on a critical attitude that was the key to or lock on the door of emotional and physical health.

In 1975, I became president of a nonprofit public foundation and its subsidiary, the International Society for Advanced Education, inspired by leading health scientists. We established a pilot international learning center in Sarasota, Florida, devoted to continuing medical education, stress management, and high-level behavior programs primarily for the practicing health professions. This activity continued for three years and greatly enhanced my awareness of the relationship between the mind and body.

In addition to input from deans of continuing medical education and faculty members of the University of Pittsburgh, Harvard University, University of Florida, University of Nebraska, University of California, and the University of Texas, there are four other individuals whose input has had a marked effect upon my research efforts: Dr. Hans Selye, pioneer in stress research and president of the International

Institute for Stress, Montreal, Canada; Dr. Joel Elkes, former psychiatrist-in-chief, the Johns Hopkins University, Baltimore, Maryland; Dr. Robert Eliot, member of the Board of Governors of the American College of Cardiology and president of the International Stress Foundation, Omaha, Nebraska; and Dr. Herbert Benson, associate professor of medicine, Harvard Medical School, Boston, Massachusetts.

In 1978, I returned to La Jolla, California, to devote full time to lecturing, consulting, and researching on healthy human behavior. During the past three years, I have been counselling and studying United States and Australian Olympic athletes, Superbowl football players, corporate executives, salesmen, educators, women's and youth organizations and institutions, attempting to verify and expand on my theories concerning attitudes.

I currently appear at large public rallies with figures such as Dr. Norman Vincent Peale, Paul Harvey, Dr. Robert Schuller, Art Linkletter, Earl Nightingale, W. Clement Stone, and Zig Ziglar. I also conduct management seminars, as a visiting scholar and fellow of the University of Southern California, with commentators like Eric Sevareid and Howard K. Smith. In order to keep abreast of economic and political attitudes, I currently am a regular public forum panelist with Ronald Reagan, Milton Friedman, Alan Greenspan, Howard Ruff, Gerald Ford, William Simon, Robert Bleiberg, and William F. Buckley, Jr.

WHY DID I WRITE THIS BOOK?

Ever since childhood, I've been obsessed by the observation that real success in life has no apparent relationship to

INTRODUCTION

a gifted birth, talent, or intelligence quotient. How can we account for identical twins born and raised in a ghetto, with a prostitute mother and an alcoholic father, where one stays in the ghetto and grows up like Mom and Dad, and the other child becomes a major-league baseball legend and a national youth leader? Or, how can we account for two children raised by educated, nurturing parents in a fine neighborhood, where one becomes a circuit court judge, and the other goes to prison for drug peddling?

My own boyhood environment was a seesaw of confusions: love, divorce, encouragement, and insecurity. As I have matured into a groping, hoping, mate-parent-breadwinner-citizen-human, I have applied my research to my own life, which for more than half of my years had professionally, domestically, and internally been a roller coaster of victories and defeats.

The results have been amazing. I am succeeding across the board. My career has mushroomed. My personal and family life are exceptionally rewarding and happy. My six children seem motivated, well-adjusted, and don't crave external stimulants to feel high on life. My wife and I love and respect each other and truly like being around each other. I feel few distressful emotions, enjoy good health, and have learned to convert the stress I used to endure into productive energy for achievement. I relish life and the people who share it with me. As an investigator, I believe I have identified some fundamental denominators that appear to be common in people who become so uncommonly successful in reaching their goals.

Today, my father manages a storage warehouse and lives in Santa Monica. To me, he does that as a hobby; his real vocation is as one of the world's greatest philosophers. My mother lives in a mobile home in San Diego and devotes her time to helping the less fortunate. How fortunate they are to have her.

This book is my way of saying "thank you" to my parents while they live. Although neither graduated from college, nor found fortune or fame, nor real self-actualization, in my eyes, they are real, genuine "winners." They gave me the first hint that there is A WINNER'S EDGE, a way of viewing life that is the critical attitude for success.

WHO IS THIS BOOK FOR?

This book is not for the super-champions who are seeking perfection, nor for the manipulators or intimidators. It is for you to use in putting yourself together in your own special version of the game of life. It contains, in my opinion, practical insights into experiences and time-tested attitudes for success, which are applicable whether you are a business executive, mechanic, professional, homemaker, parent, athlete, or student. It's for you if you have never really succeeded, if you just want more of the same success you now enjoy, or if you have made it, lost it, and would like to get it again and keep it.

The object of this book is to provide the reader with the most critical and important elements that develop and sustain an attitude toward life that results in success for the individual. It is not about gurus, cosmic energy, ESP, or some pseudointellectual or cult movement. At a time in our history when we are being bombarded by the search for something else as a panacea for our individual and col-

INTRODUCTION

lective frustrations, this book offers a "back to the basics" approach to healthy behavior, supported by current research in the health sciences and by anecdotal evidence from the lives of "winners" in many different arenas of society.

WINNERS

WINNING has a new definition for individuals and organizations in the game of life. It used to mean beating the others and being Number One. Winning signified standing victoriously over a fallen adversary—"the survival of the fittest." As we enter the final decades of this century, it is obvious that the very nature of "winning" must change.

THE DOUBLE-WIN

The real winners in the present and future world arena will be more often the champions of "cooperation," rather than the champions of "competition." While power to maintain access to resources will continue to prevail, "the survival of the fittest" philosophy will give way to what Jonas Salk describes in his recent book as the "survival of the wisest" philosophy of understanding, cooperation, and reason.

The "Win-Lose" playbook that suggests that there must be a loser for every winner, that winning by intimidation is fashionable, is obsolete. The "Win-Win" playbook is the only one that can endure. "Win-Win" means: "If I help you win, then I win too!" The real winners in life get what they want by helping others get what they want. Independence has been replaced by interdependence. There are too many people, too few resources, and too delicate a balance between nature and technology to produce winners in isolation today.

There will be no lasting peace on earth until there is a "piece of pie" in every mouth. It is the expectation of tomorrow's bigger, better pie, from which everyone will taste a larger piece, that prevents people from competing and struggling to the end over the division of today's pie. As eager students in the art of winning our individual games of life, we must, at the onset, face the inescapable fact that we as individuals are a vital but single organ of a larger body of human beings in the world. The one cannot succeed, or even survive for long anymore, without the others.

WHO ARE THE WINNERS?

Winners, in my opinion, are those individuals who in a very natural, free-flowing way seem to consistently get what they want from life by providing valuable service to others. They put themselves together across the board—in their personal, professional, and community lives. They set and achieve goals that benefit others as well as themselves. You don't have to get lucky to win at life, nor do you have to knock other people down or gain at the expense of others.

WINNERS

Winning is taking the talent or potential you were born with, and have since developed, and using it fully toward a purpose that makes you feel worthwhile according to your own internal standards. Happiness, then, is the natural by-product of living a worthwhile life. It is not a goal to be chased after or sought.

Happiness is the natural experience of winning your own self-respect, as well as the respect of others. Happiness should not be confused with indulgence, escapism, or hedonistic pleasure-seeking. You can't drink, inhale, or snort happiness. You can't buy it, wear it, drive it, swallow it, inject it, or travel to it! Happiness is the journey, not the destination. As elusive as a butterfly, happiness comes only to those who feel it without chasing it.

THE WINNER'S EDGE

There seems to be only a fine line between the top five percent of the real achievers, the real winners in society, and the rest of the pack. I call this fine line of demarcation "the Winner's Edge." When I think of the Winner's Edge, I'm reminded of the difference between simple boiling water and powerful steam, which is used to power the giant steam catapults that used to launch my Navy jet aircraft from the flight deck of aircraft carriers. When water is heated to 211 degrees Fahrenheit, it is simply boiling water. However, when the temperature reaches 212 degrees, only one degree higher, the water is converted into steam which is powerful enough to hurtle 60 tons of steel from a dead stop to 120 miles an hour in five seconds.

THE WINNER'S EDGE

On the professional golf tour in the United States, only a few shots separate the top money winners in golf from the rest of the tour. In baseball, the American and National League batting champions every year actually only hit safely about 20 or 30 more times in an entire season than those who didn't make the top ten in the batting average finals. Just a few strokes of the bat in a different way separates the true champion from the average professional. In the Olympic games, the difference between the gold-medal winner in the 100-meter dash in track and the fourth-place nonmedal winner is often only two-tenths of a second. And so the Winning Edge is only a degree here and a few strokes there, or a few swings here and a couple of tenths of a second there.

In the National Football League on any given Sunday, any team in the league can beat another team, depending on its mental preparation before the game. The talent in professional football is so nearly equal that the score at the end of the final gun is a matter of inches and split-second timing.

What is true on the athletic field of competition seems also to hold true in every other walk of life. The real leaders in business, in the professional community, in education, in government, and in the home also seem to draw upon a special cutting edge that separates them from the rest of society. This cutting edge can be measured in inches, tenths of a second, ounces, pennies, or degrees. When we speak of degrees, we're not speaking of educational degrees. We're speaking of degrees of persistence, degrees of effectiveness, and degrees of positive awareness.

The Winner's Edge is not in a gifted birth, a high IQ, or in talent. Talent is cheap; you can buy it and recruit it, and it's everywhere. The world is full of talented alcoholics. The

Winner's Edge is not in education. Education is not cheap, but it is for sale and for hire if you have the time and the money. You can get your B.S., M.B.A. or Ph.D. and panel your den with diplomas, but the world is full of educated derelicts unable to relate to supportive roles with others. The Winner's Edge is all in the attitude! Not aptitude—attitude is the criterion for success. But you can't buy an attitude for a million dollars. Attitudes are not for sale.

GREATNESS OUT OF ADVERSITY

All individuals are not born equal. Some are cursed and some are blessed with their hereditary uniforms. Equality is not nature's way. The equal right to become unequal by choice seems to be the natural cycle. All environments do not breed and nurture the winning spirit. Yet, how often we are witness to living examples of greatness that spring out of adversity.

Some individuals are born with much more going for them: They come from wealthy parents, beautiful parents, talented, or intelligent parents. Many children have been encouraged and nurtured by winning parents, outstanding teachers, coaches, and friends who gave them feelings of worthiness. But there is an amazing historical pattern that is almost contradictory, and that is the pattern that some of the offspring of the richest, most beautiful, most prominent and talented people have become losers, unable to live up to their heritage and unable to accept themselves or to perform effectively on their own. This may be because they had so much going for them at the start that they developed no inner drive to take them forward. Yet, some children from the most backward, discouraging beginnings have grown into outstanding winners and top achievers in every walk of life. *Attitude is the answer. Your attitude toward your potential is either the key to or the lock on the door of personal fulfillment.*

In the studies of winners who have pulled themselves from relatively modest beginnings and who have remained at the top in their lives, this critical attitude for success seems to be the common denominator. Benjamin Franklin, Thomas Edison, Golda Meir, and Margaret Thatcher all have been associated with early feelings of positive attitudes. Look at Helen Keller, who, though blind and deaf, dedicated her life to helping the less fortunate. And Albert Einstein, who failed his college entrance exams, but went on to develop the theory of relativity. And Galileo, who was groomed to be a tailor but dropped out of the factory into scientific history. Manachem Begin of Israel, who began as a street urchin in a Polish ghetto. And the desert peasant boy, who was falsely imprisoned for treason as a young officer in Egypt's wasteland, and, after several years of confinement in cell 54, went on to become Egypt's president, Anwar Sadat.

Perhaps the most dramatic example in history of the successful attitude and the ability to take a record of defeat and use a healthy attitude to achieve victory is in reviewing the professional accomplishments and track record of Abraham Lincoln. He lost his job in 1832. He was defeated for the legislature, also in 1832. He failed in business in 1833. He was elected to the legislature in 1834. His sweetheart died in 1835. Lincoln suffered a nervous breakdown in 1836. He was defeated for speaker in 1838. He was defeated for nomination for congress in 1843. Lincoln was elected to congress in 1846.

WINNERS

He lost his renomination for congress in 1848. He was rejected for land officer in 1849. Lincoln was defeated for the senate in 1854. He was defeated for the nomination for vice-president of the United States in 1856. He was again defeated for senate in 1858. Abraham Lincoln was elected president of the United States in 1860. He had the Winner's Edge, that critical attitude for success.

THE MALIBU ROCK

One of the more recent, true illustrations of the power of different attitudes on events in peoples' lives has an Australian flavor. Not long ago, I appeared on the Sunday Christian television program, *Hour of Power,* created by Dr. Robert Schuller, founder and pastor of the Garden Grove Community Church in Garden Grove, California. Robert Schuller speaks weekly to millions of "possibility thinkers" who make up his worldwide television congregation. The day I appeared on his show, I gave him his sermon for the morning about an Australian youth with a magnificent obsession: The Malibu Rock.

In July of 1979, my wife and I were on a speaking tour throughout Australia and, by coincidence, happened to be in Perth, West Australia, at the same time as NASA's orbiting satellite laboratory, Skylab, came to its fiery end after years of valuable service. We noticed two equally intense, but opposite moods among the Australians. Many of the Australians we met were uneasy, apprehensive, and some were frightened by the prospects of Skylab falling on their homes or on their heads. Like Henny Penny and Ducky Lucky, they ran around declaring to all within earshot that the sky was falling. "What if it lands on us?" they lamented, helplessly. "It could kill us all. Why don't they do something to guarantee our safety? Why us? Why couldn't it come down in Russia, China, or in New York City?"

The other group of Australians we observed were the optimists. They were excited about the prospects of witnessing the re-entry of the space vehicle. When it streaked across the western sky and put on a magnificent post-Fourth of July fireworks display like the Aurora Borealis, they clapped and said: "I hope a piece of it comes down on my farm, I'd like a souvenir from outer space. I can tell my grandchildren I've got a hunk of history, just like an antique crank off an old model-T Ford." Or: "I hope it falls in my yard. I understand the first person who gets to a San Francisco radio station with a verified piece of Skylab gets a $10,000 reward!"

THE WINNER'S EDGE AUSTRALIAN STYLE

This polarity of hope and despair over the "news of the hour" reminded me of a true story that involves an Australian young man who, to me, characterizes the attitudes I am trying to portray in this book.

Brett Livingstone Strong was born on October 31, 1953, in Junee, Australia. His father was an artist who gave his own palette to his son when Brett was only four years old. Shortly thereafter, his father was killed in a water-skiing accident, while in his early thirties. Still a young boy, Brett faced his first major attitude crossroads. Should he look back and say, "Why us, Lord?" Or should he look forward and say, "Now it's up to me, Lord!"

Brett painted and then sculpted his way through Sydney Grammar School, with never any formal training in art. In Blakehurst High School, New South Wales, he topped the state competition with his sculpture, *Water Reeds,* which he fashioned of fiberglass and foam coated with iridescent sea-green enamel. In 1971, at eighteen, he was the youngest sculptor ever to be exhibited at the New South Wales Art Gallery. (His work, *Torso of Woman,* has the distinction of being the only sculpture ever stolen from the gallery!) His prize-winning oil painting, *Australia,* depicting an aborigine gazing with wonder at the futuristic Sydney Opera House against the vastness of the country, was chosen to hang in the Sydney Opera House when Queen Elizabeth went to Australia for the Gala Opening in 1973.

Also in 1973, the owner of a stone mason yard gave him a three-foot-high marble headstone, which every professional knew was too fragile to carve. Brett saw a beautiful woman in the piece of marble. He was told his design was impossible to create, because in carving the woman's delicate arms and legs the marble would surely shatter when he tried to separate them from the main body of the sculpture. This is what winners love—to be told that what they have envisioned is impossible! Brett exhibited *Creation of Woman* in Sydney and Brisbane, Australia, and sold it in 1977 to a Swedish art collector for $60,000. This financed his world travelling exhibition, which brought him to the United States.

Enter the Malibu Rock and the major attitude crossroad in the life of Brett Livingstone Strong.

23

THE ROCK IS FALLING!

It had been raining in Southern California for most of the first two weeks in February 1979. Mud and rocks were falling down the slopes, most of them unnoticed and unpublicized. However, a 116-ton rock that perched a little over 180 feet above Pacific Coast Highway in Malibu, between Topanga Canyon Boulevard and Malibu Canyon Road, was being noticed and would soon become very well publicized indeed.

Some homeowners who live in the 19700 block of Pacific Coast Highway in Malibu noticed the rock directly above them. One of them was film producer Robert Radnitz. He and his neighbors in the row of costly houses on the beach feared it would come crashing down, sliding on the mud all around it, and causing property damage and injuries—or even deaths—on the highway. Radnitz sent a telegram to the California Department of Transportation, holding them directly responsible for anything that happened because of the rock. That got action in a hurry. The state ordered the owners of the property on which the rock balanced, The Iranian Import Co., to have the rock removed immediately. When they would not or could not, the State hired a construction company to remove it. The successful bid was for $92,648.

It was supposed to be an open-and-shut job shortly after midnight on Valentine's Day. The highway would be closed for a few hours at most. A net would be raised by helicopter to be fastened to the rock by a crew in bulldozers; then the helicopter would gently lower the rock to the highway, where a cushion of mud would have been spread to break its fall and prevent its rolling onto the houses. Simple enough!

WINNERS

A crowd began to gather as the road was closed and the dirt was spread. Shortly after dawn, three Caterpillar D-9 tractors started up the hill. It was well past noon before they were in place. Workers had trouble getting the 30-by-30 foot, 2,500 pound net laced together. A twin-turbine jet helicopter picked up the net and draped it over the rock with no difficulty. The tractors, tied together in tandem, began pulling.

The rock did not move.

All during the first day, the crowd of onlookers had increased until it had the appearance of a huge party. Hundreds of newsmen arrived on the scene to watch the drama unfold. That night one news photographer got stuck on a ledge near the rock and had to be rescued by helicopter. The crowd cheered.

The rock did not move.

Geological engineers watched the rock all night long. Some said they saw it move. Others simply saw things.

Brett Livingstone Strong watched the rock, too. "When I look at a piece of stone or marble, I feel I can penetrate it with my mind and can actually see the form the sculpture should take. I feel the sculpture is inside the stone, just waiting for me to peel off the outer surfaces. I wanted that rock in Malibu the first time I heard about it on the news. So I went out there and arranged to buy it."

The Iranian Import Co. said Brett could have the rock for nothing, but the construction company said it was their property. So Brett purchased it for $100, provided he would take full responsibility for moving it.

The following day, Brett watched with the crowd as the rock was bombarded with 32,000 gallons of water from a 400 foot fire hose.

25

The rock refused to move.

Someone was heard to exclaim in exasperation, "The damn thing is welded to a steel beam down the middle of it."

"Superman" arrived at the party that day. The crowd enjoyed the carnival atmosphere. Newspaper stories poured forth with headlines such as "Rock Around the Clock" and "Watch on the Rock." It became a television star, much more popular than the "pet rock." At least one TV newsman would quip, "Cue the Rock!" One enterprising entrepreneur announced he would manufacture "rock T-shirts."

The rock did not move.

Finally, just before sundown, on Friday, February 16, 1979, after a herculean effort with a one-inch steel cable and skiploader, the Malibu Rock came tumbling down, crashing through the net holding it, breaking chains and shooting sparks as it fell 180 feet to the mud cushion, landing smack in the middle of Pacific Coast Highway.

About 2 A.M. on February 18, Pacific Coast Highway finally opened to traffic again. It had been closed for two and one-half days. The loss in business revenues, salaries, and school per diem funds had swelled the overall cost to well over a million dollars for removal of The Malibu Rock. Its name was changed to "The Malibu Million-Dollar Rock."

Everyone was laughing at the young Australian, who they thought was out of his mind to purchase the 116-ton rock that had become the joke of Malibu. Brett wasn't laughing, nor paying any attention. He was busy examining the rock, with the precision of a master diamond cutter, already envisioning the work that was about to be born. From the moment he saw the rock, he didn't see it as a "public menace" as the others did. He saw it as a "public masterpiece!"

On March 2, 1979, Brett's "white elephant" was moved onto a grassy knoll in front of the Century Square shopping center in Century City, 20 miles away. The Century City Cultural Commission and the Century Square Merchant's Association welcomed Brett in his endeavor to carve his magnificent obsession out of "The Malibu Million-Dollar Rock."

BRETT'S MAGNIFICENT OBSESSION

It was to be a man's face, a special man's face. Rugged, stubborn, weathered with time, and, like the rock itself, tough to bring down, a monument in his own right.

At the time Brett began his work, this man was engaged in the greatest struggle of his lifetime, nearby at the UCLA Medical Center. Brett had seen, in an instant, the parallel between the Malibu Rock and the man.

Every television station in Los Angeles covered the story —the rock had finally moved. Newspapers and magazines sent reporters to "follow that rock." As Brett worked with his pneumatic jack-hammer and chisels, each day brought changes in "the stranger's face." Crowds came every day to watch, chat, ask questions, and marvel at the sheer determination of the young Australian. Schools sent art students to see a sculptor in action. Most sculptors work off a scale model. They use a boom on top of the model and another on top of the rock and measure by means of a plumb line for accuracy. In this manner, they know exactly where each cut is to be made for the eyes, nose, chin, and other areas of the sculpture. Brett worked only from photographs and his feel-

27

ing for the character of the subject, and he worked in full view of the public every day, which is rarely attempted.

After eight weeks of total commitment, the work of art was completed. How was Brett to have known that the man for whom he had labored would not live to see the unveiling? For the person whose incredible, remarkable likeness he had created was "the Duke"—John Wayne.

"I chose to honor John Wayne, as he represented to me a great love of life. He is a man who strived to reach the top in his career; through sheer effort, he succeeded. He has given the world enjoyment with his entertainment, financial assistance, and his deep personal interest in others. I admire John Wayne, a man of strength and courage, like the rock itself. I even saved the first chip for him."

What has happened since "The John Wayne Rock" was conceived and achieved is so unbelievable, I checked it out to make certain it was really true. Here's the punch line of the story: Like Henny Penny and Ducky Lucky the California homeowners looked up and saw a menace. "That rock will fall and crush us. Bring it down!" But it was basically a "good" rock and hadn't planned to fall on anyone, for it had been thrust upward eons ago, and more of it was beneath the surface than that which met their fearful eyes. It cost the taxpayers of the state of California one million dollars for them to get their wish!

Everyone laughed when the young Australian bought it for a hundred dollars. After all, it cost him another twenty-five thousand or so just to haul it away!

The laughter sounded hollow with the dramatic unveiling of the amazing bust of John Wayne seventy days after "The Malibu Rock" had come crashing down from its sentry post.

WINNERS

The laughter turned into a gasping roar of approval when the announcement hit the press that Tom G. Murphy of Scottsdale, Arizona, had purchased the rock from Brett Livingstone Strong for one million dollars! *Winning is all in the attitude!* One set of attitudes brought the rock down to the tune of a one million dollar fiasco. The Winner's Edge, another kind of attitude, created a masterpiece, resulting in a one million dollar bonanza for a young Australian sculptor and perhaps several million dollars more for Tom Murphy and the John Wayne Cancer Center.

As for the rock, it's enjoying its new face and notoriety. It's been bringing joy to thousands of John Wayne fans on exhibition at the world-famous Mann's Chinese Theatre in Hollywood. And there's a rumor circulating that the rock may soon head for its permanent home back up on the hill over Pacific Coast Highway again. Only this time it might be placed just down the road, in the J. Paul Getty Museum of Fine Art!

Brett Livingstone Strong, like so many other winners, has the critical attitude for success, the attitude that makes one realize it makes little difference what is actually happening in life, it is how you take it that counts. In the chapters that follow, this Winner's Edge is separated into what I consider to be its most critical elements: self-honesty; self-esteem; a creative self-image; positive self-expectancy; and self-dimension.

SELF-HONESTY

THE first and most important element of that critical attitude for success that makes up the Winner's Edge is self-honesty. Self-honesty is the ability to step back from the canvas of life and take a good look at yourself as you relate to your environmental, physical, mental, and spiritual world. Self-honesty is the ability to accept yourself as a unique, imperfect, changing, and growing individual and to recognize your own vast potential as well as your limitations.

LIFE IS A "DO-IT-TO-YOURSELF" PROGRAM

One of the most important aspects of self-honesty in the Winner's Edge is that winners take full responsibility for determining their actions in their own lives. They believe in

31

cause and effect and have the philosophy that life is a "do-it-to-yourself" program.

Many people refuse to face the truth in the mirror of their lives on a daily basis and prefer to hide behind the belief that fate, luck, biorhythm, or, possibly, their astrological sign have shaped the outcome of their lives. These people, who feel that life is mostly determined by circumstance, predestination, or being at the right place at the right time, are more likely to give in to doubt and fear. Those who cannot make up their minds for fear of making the wrong choice, vacillating in indecision, simply do not achieve their goals—a requisite for success. Rather, they take their place among the rank and file, trudging along in mediocrity.

People who are aware that they exert control over what happens to them in life are happier and are able to choose more appropriate responses to whatever occurs. All individuals are what they are and where they are as a composite result of all their own doings. It is true that we are all God-created, but we are also "self-molded." Although our innate characteristics and environment are given to us initially, the decisions we make determine whether we win or lose our particular game of life.

GOD DEALS, YOU PLAY!

Voltaire likened life to a game of cards. Each player must accept the cards life deals him or her. But once they are in hand, he or she alone must decide how to play the cards in order to win the game. The writer, John Erskine, put it a little differently when he wrote: "Though we sometimes speak of a primrose path, we all know that a bad life is just as difficult, just as full of work, obstacles, and hardships, as a good one. The only choice is the kind of life one would care to spend one's efforts on."

Whether you are a bum on skid row or a happy individual, you can pat yourself on the back, taking the credit or the blame for your place in life. You took over control from your parents when you were very young and have been in the driver's seat ever since. I didn't realize until I was 35 that I'm behind the wheel in my life. I thought it was the government, inflation, the energy crisis, and my heritage. I used to think that as a Gemini, I was destined to be creative but non-specific.

CONTROL BEGINS AT BIRTH

I should have taken a hint from one of my daughters when she was only eleven months old. She was in her high chair for dinner, and I decided she should eat some nourishing strained squash. I tasted it to test the temperature. It was bland and not too exciting, but I knew it was good for her. I held the little curved spoon out and gently entreated, "Open up, honey, Daddy has some yummy squash for you." She stared coldly at me and clamped her mouth shut in passive defiance. Although she was unable to speak, had she been able to talk she certainly would have said, "Go ahead, fatso, why don't you eat it." Being in total control of the situation, I simply pressed her cheeks firmly with two fingers, thus forcing her mouth open. I then neatly inserted the spoonful of squash into her mouth and quietly, but sternly, ordered, "Go on, swallow it; it's good for you." She spit it out all over my face! She had decided at eleven months old she did not like the taste of strained squash. She is 21 years old and for some strange reason does not like squash.

Children do begin to take control of their lives at an early age. Many children learn how to control their parents' lives as well, long before they know how to talk in complete sentences. Whining receives attention. Crying receives consolation. Begging gets goodies. Tantrums create havoc. It's easy to incite Mommy against Daddy and sit back and watch the show.

There is a disturbing trend among young parents all over the United States today to be at the mercy of their babies and little tots. It is especially noticeable on cross-country trips aboard commercial airliners, where the parents are not able to exert enough control to even keep seat belts on their children long enough for take off and landing, let alone to sit down for a complete meal at a table in a restaurant. The same trend is spreading throughout the school system in this country, from nursery school through high school.

I know one couple, both graduates of one of our major universities, who have so little control over their child that to get their five-year-old to bed while I was visiting, they had to put granola cookies on the stairs as an incentive, so he would eat all the way to his bedroom on the second floor. Parents who subordinate their lives to their children, regardless of age, are irresponsible, in a sense, and will find that their children will have difficulty later on facing the realities and responsibilities of life outside the demand system they enjoy at home.

WHO'S IN CHARGE HERE?

As a first step in developing the aspects of self-honesty in the critical attitude for success, we need to ask ourselves the question: Are you steering your ship, or are you a victim to the ill or fair winds of fate? Are you a puppet dangling on the strings of your heredity and environment? Are there a lot of things you have to do in life that have been forced upon you? People who feel they have to do things usually forfeit many available options and alternatives and lose control of their lives in the process.

Traditional psychotherapy has in many ways been a great disservice to the improvement of the healthy outlook of people undergoing treatment. By replaying the past and dredging up memories and by looking back at the probable causes of deviant behavior, little more has been done other than focusing on that behavior, rationalizing it, and perhaps even fixing the blame for it on an environmental or hereditary condition.

There has been a positive breakthrough in psychology in recent years, which was first led by Dr. Abraham Maslow, prior to his death, and by Carl Rodgers, William Glasser, Viktor Frankl, and many other prominent humanists. This new movement, which is optimistic about human growth and potential and looks forward instead of backward, is commonly referred to as "responsibility psychology." It holds that irresponsibility and valuelessness lead to abnormal behavior, neurosis, and mental deterioration. Treatment of individuals suffering from these symptoms includes showing them that they need not be hung up on the past, but they are responsible for their present actions as well as their future behavior. Psychiatrist William Glasser and others have found that when a neurotic individual is helped to look at situations realistically and assume personal responsibility, the prognosis for recovery is good. In case after case, they verify that responsible self-honesty leads to sound mental health.

WINNERS MAKE IT HAPPEN! LOSERS LET IT HAPPEN!

The winning human being realizes that everything in life is volition—even being alive. Everything is something *I decide to do,* and there is nothing *I have to do.* You don't have to go to work, pay taxes, have babies, or even get up in the morning. You could go on welfare, try to beat the Internal Revenue Service, go to prison, stay single, or stay in bed. You decide to do things because they are profitable to you and the best choice among the alternatives available to help you reach your goals.

People who have to do things are irresponsible. They are dishonest and are not in control of their lives. They are puppets caught in the habit of letting life happen to them. Losers let it happen; winners make it happen.

In his book, *Self-Renewal,* John Gardner states that winning individuals do not leave the development of their potential to chance. They pursue it honestly, systematically, and look forward to an endless dialogue between their potentials and the claims of life—not only the claims they encounter, but the claims they invent. Daily, thousands of individuals are finding that there is a bright new world out there to be discovered and are demonstrating Gardner's statement that "we don't know we've been imprisoned until we've broken out."

THE STATUE OF RESPONSIBILITY: OUR NEW DECLARATION OF INDEPENDENCE

We are not only victims of habits. In a very real sense, each of us becomes a prisoner of hundreds of restrictions of our own making.

Teen-agers have a strong need to conform to the standards of their group. While they may feel that their special way of grooming is an act of independence, on the contrary, their styles and activities adhere very strictly to the peer code. Those who refuse to be responsible and honest for their own deeds, looking to others for their behavior cues, have not reached maturity. Unfortunately, many adults spend their entire lives at this level of immaturity.

As we grow into adulthood, we make decisions that progressively narrow our opportunities and alternatives. We seek only a few friends out of the thousands with whom we rub elbows, usually people with whom we agree, thus limiting our input of fresh ideas. We choose our educational level, which in turn determines to a great extent our jobs and associates. From day to day, comfortable in our safe, established way, we seek the paths of least resistance. The responsible people look at the shackles they've placed upon themselves by apathy and lack of imagination and, in a moment

37

of truth, decry their predicament. Making a declaration of independence, they assert their option to choose and assume their rightful role of personal honesty.

In her last book, famed anthropologist, the late Margaret Mead, calls personal honesty and responsibility our most important development and the notion that we are the product of our environment, our biggest sin. There should be a Statue of Responsibility standing in Los Angeles or San Francisco harbor to match the Statue of Liberty. Without individual responsibility, there can be no enduring liberty or freedom in any society. We will be free only as long as we can use freedom responsibly.

THE LAW OF CAUSE AND EFFECT IS FOREVER THE RULER

Earl Nightingale, in his radio broadcasts and written works, has reminded us through the years of one of the great natural laws of the universe: the law of cause and effect. For every cause, there will be an effect nearly equal in intensity. If we make good use of our minds, skills, and talents, these will become apparent in our outer lives. And, if we make the best use of our time, this, too, will give us a great advantage, for we know that scarcely one in a thousand individuals ever puts his or her time to anywhere near its potential good use.

This is being true to ourselves—taking control, accepting responsibility. In the final analysis, we are the only ones from whom we can steal time and accomplishment. We are the only true field judges in our own daily Superbowls in life.

Now that we have stepped back from our lives and made

an honest appraisal that life is a do-it-to-yourself project, we are ready to take the next step in developing that critical attitude for success. We are ready to make an honest evaluation as to how we are looking at life and how honest we have been in measuring our potential against the vast potential in our world. In order to make an honest evaluation of where we stand in society, we first must determine how society is being served to us via every means of human expression.

WHAT'S WRONG VS. WHAT'S RIGHT

One of the most glaring reasons why we have such a difficult time seeing the abundance of potential in our own lives that enables us to be real winners is that the media is bombarding us with the "wrong doings" of society rather than the "right doings." ABC newscaster, Paul Harvey, says that he is appalled by the way the news of the world is portrayed on a daily basis to individuals in our society, with all the focus on deviant behavior rather than on what's happening that is right.

Beyond the factual revelation of the ills of society, in order that it might be improved, there is an alarming focus today on deviant behavior and the acts of a mentally deranged minority in the world. So powerful and frequent are the slick, dramatic portrayals of the most revolting human biographies, that society is methodically being transformed by example into a working model for losers. Books, movies, television, magazines, newspapers, and coffee klatches all bombard us with stark brutality alluding to the new realism in our society—thus the focus of our daily conversation on

39

Teheran, Jonestown, the weird occult, sexual aberrations, violence, crime, traffic accidents, and airplane crashes.

WE'RE GLAD WE WEREN'T THE VICTIMS

Paul Harvey suggests that the reason we as individuals are so morbidly curious whenever we read about human indignities is that "we're glad we weren't the victims and so bad news becomes good news in reverse. The fire that burned another person may be the one that warmed our own gratefulness that we weren't the victim for the day." By reading, talking, and viewing the tragedies of others, we are able to justify our own bland, uneventful, and less-than-productive lives.

TELEVISION: THE MODEL FOR LOSERS

We all hope that the bombardment of nightly television situation comedies and violent cops and robbers shows, ranging from incest to homosexuality, has no effect on our own lives and the lives of our children. How dumb can we get? If 60-second commercials cost more than $100,000 for one minute of prime time just to try to give us a subliminal hint to buy a product or service, can you imagine the impact of 48 minutes of situation comedies and hour after hour of deviant behavior in the name of entertainment served to our children who watch day after day in a semistupor?

SELF-HONESTY

By the time children reach age five today, they have been subjected to some 3,000 hours of television programming. If a commercial can get you to buy a new toy, you can believe that the rest of the show can get you to buy a losing lifestyle as a normal way of life. By concentrating on what is wrong with society, we find ourselves unable to spend much time thinking about what we are doing right or what we can do right. We become very depressed, we lose our real incentives and excitement about life and see society as an historical pattern of losing, from Mayan and Grecian times, to the Roman Empire, up to the present. We spend much of our time gleefully predicting the coming of the end.

NOW IS OUR BEST HOUR

In developing our critical attitude for success, our self-honesty needs to tell us that this is the best time to be living in society. There is more opportunity today and in our foreseeable lifetime than in any other time in history. We have managed to conquer most of the infectious diseases that can attack and destroy our lives from the outside. Recent breakthroughs in the production of Interferon may deter the growth of cancer as well as virus infections, which have plagued us since our beginnings. Through nutritional, medical, surgical, and pharmaceutical intervention, we have been able to increase our life span well beyond 70 years. And the prospects look good for pushing the average life span up toward 80 years in the next decade.

There is more freedom in society than ever before and more opportunity for one to express one's own talents and opinions. Physical fitness is a way of life today, as evidenced by the fact that just to compete in the Junior Olympics as a teen-ager one has to break Johnny Weismuller's world-record gold-medal attempt in the 200-meter free-style swimming event. Teens and preteens today are breaking the world records set by Olympic champions of less than 20 years ago.

Yet, everywhere we look, there seems to be a crisis. First, it was the Cuban missile crisis, then the crisis of Watergate, next the Middle East crisis, the energy crisis, the Iranian crisis, the Chrysler crisis, and, for each of us, the middle-age crisis.

CRISIS EQUALS OPPORTUNITY

In the Chinese language, the symbol for crisis is the combination of "danger" and "opportunity." Through the centuries, the Chinese have come to know that crisis and opportunity are synonymous. The current energy crisis is one of the greatest opportunities for Western civilization since the industrial revolution. Just as the Russians' orbiting of the Sputnik satellites touched off the space-technology crisis in the United States and spawned the Apollo program and Neil Armstrong's walk on the moon, so has the recent energy crisis given new birth to alternate sources of energy to power our lives as we approach the 21st century.

Using the technology of laser fusion and water, the prospects of one-sixteenth of an inch of San Francisco Bay powering the western United States for 350 years is not a pipe dream. Liquid-hydrogen engines are already in the testing phase on the various salt flats of the automobile proving grounds. Liquid hydrogen, the same fuel that powered the Apollo spacecraft to the moon, may well power our private and commercial transportation vehicles of the future. The most exciting thing about liquid-hydrogen-powered vehicles is that the exhaust from these engines burns cleaner than the air above Pikes Peak. It may be possible that in the year 2020, in the city of Los Angeles, there will be ten million liquid-hydrogen-powered vehicles. They will suck the smog out of the basin, like vacuum cleaners, and make the air that comes out of these vehicles cleaner than the air that went in. It will thereby solve the smog problem and give us the ability to see the mountains of San Bernardino which we haven't seen since 1949.

There is also energy from alcohol, energy from deep thermal rocks near the center of the earth. Energy from the sun, the conversion of coal into petroleum. Battery power, garbage power, and there is still hope for nuclear power.

We are very fortunate that electricity was not brought to us via a destructive weapon in the same way that nuclear power was first introduced to us via the atomic bomb at Hiroshima. Had the first product of electricity been the electric chair, you can be sure that today we'd be afraid to plug in our toasters and appliances because of the way we concentrate on the negatives, rather than turning problems into opportunities.

The same the type of technology at Los Alamos Scientific Labs that Teller Oppenheimer, in the Manhattan Project, used to develop the atomic bomb and split the atom is now being used to split the atom into even smaller particles for the benefit of mankind, rather than for the destruction. The linear accelerator at Los Alamos is splitting the atoms down to small particles called mesons, and these meson particles have a very short life span. When these particles are propelled into the human body at the exact location of a tumor, there is a good prospect that the radiation treatment of the tumor will not have as adverse effects on the other organs of the body as in traditional radiation treatment of cancer. Thus an invention for destruction has been turned into an invention for the saving and lengthening of human life. A crisis is turned into an opportunity.

UNTAPPED ENVIRONMENTAL ABUNDANCE

The Winner's Edge means an honest evaluation that there is more abundance in the environment and in society than you and I could ever utilize in a thousand lifetimes. We look, but we rarely see the tremendous abundance everywhere. How many sunrises and sunsets have you watched this month? How many good books have you read? How many informative audio-cassette programs have you listened to this month? Did you use your Betamax to record all the National Geographic specials and classic theater presentations? When was your last trip to Australia to watch the koala climb the eucalyptus tree? Is your education continuing? There are a number of college-degree programs that you can accomplish almost completely by correspondence, which require only one week or one month on campus. How's your sailboat? How's your family? Do you realize that parents today spend less than 60 seconds a day alone with each child, one-on-one, at a time when the child is most receptive to encouraging inputs? Have you fed or clothed an orphan this month? How's your retirement income relative to inflation? Are you financially secure or looking forward to social security? Are you taking advantage of all the opportunities in your environmental world?

JUST ANOTHER BAD DAY

Our first step in developing the Winner's Edge is to be completely honest with the fact that society tends to dwell on the negative and serve negative inputs to us on a daily basis. From the time we wake up in the morning until the time we go to bed, there are more negative inputs.

Motivational speaker Zig Zigler says that when we wake up in the morning, we are awakened not by the crow of a rooster to herald sunrise, but we are awakened by an electronic device that we have chosen to call an *alarm* clock. So we wake up in a state of alarm and continue the rest of the day. Instead of listening to beautiful music as we prepare to go to the office, we listen to the morning news to find out what is *wrong* in the world. We read the headlines in the newspaper to find out what else is *wrong,* as we quickly drink a cup of coffee. Instead of leisurely driving to our life's career every morning with enthusiasm and excitement, we hurry through the stifling traffic because we have to go *to work.* And to be kind to ourselves during the day, because of the dull drudgery we are going through, we give ourselves a coffee *break* every hour or so just to make it tolerable. If we are unfortunate to have a minor traffic accident on the way home, we immediately call for a *wrecker,* but we've already had the wreck so what we really need is the tow truck, but our vocabulary always dwells on the negative so we call and bring the wrecker. Safely home again each evening, we take a look at the stack of mail piled on our desk and resolve ourselves to pay our *debts* tonight. Instead of paying for our purchases and our possessions, we always pay our *debts*. Then it is a dose of the early-evening news to find out what went wrong all day around the world, and then we settle down to a nice evening of TV soap operas, where the father has fallen in love with his own daughter, and the mother is secretly in love with the water softener service man. We finish it off with a rape/murder mystery, and then settle into bed with the TV turned to the eleven o'clock news, to take a final look at what went wrong in the world that day.

COPING WITH "INVISIBLE" ENTRAPMENT

No wonder we are always trying to escape from something. The Winner's Edge means adapting, instead of escaping. Adaptability is the key to success, to mental and physical health, and even the key to survival in today's world, which is full of sensory bombardment. During the past 50 years, electronic advances in telephone, television, satellites, and computerized communications have accelerated to the point where we are subjected to more information transactions in a single day, than our grandparents experienced in their entire lifetimes.

In our evolution during the past five hundred thousand years, there has been little, if any, change in our ability to cope with or adapt to our rapidly changing society. At the first hint of a dangerous or threatening confrontation from the environment, the body automatically musters its defenses in preparation for flight or fight.

Instead of a sabre-toothed tiger-a-week or a dinosaur-a-month, today it is at least one or two unwelcome or unpleasant interpersonal surprises before bedtime rolls around each night. How many complete strangers, whom you will never meet in person, got you uptight and ready to risk your life on the freeway today? Because of our steady diet of negative inputs from all of our daily and media sources, we tend to overreact like the cave dwellers, to what is happening in the environment. We flare to anger quickly and get defensive easily. Our blood pressure jumps, as our heart rate quickens, as our arteries constrict, as the adrenaline pumps, as we rush headlong into an imaginary struggle for survival, or as we run and hide from imaginary predators and volcanic eruptions. The effects of this type of daily distress or negative stress are devastating to the mental and physical health of the individual. As a result we tend to drink more, smoke more, fret more, and pop more pills to cope or escape.

Dr. Robert Eliot, member of the board of governors of the American College of Cardiology and president of the International Stress Foundation, is studying the relationship between stress and heart attacks, strokes, and other contemporary diseases. Dr. Eliot refers to the syndrome of "invisible entrapment" or the deep-seated worries, frustrations, and anxieties of people unable to cope effectively with their changing status in a changing world, as major factors in the increasing incidence of sudden death from heart attacks and other mental and physical illnesses.

The anti-anxiety drugs, increasing in use in the United States today (over 60 million tablets consumed annually), serve to reduce emotional reactions to threats of pain or failure; that is why they are taken. But, unfortunately, they also interfere with the ability to learn to tolerate these stresses. It is far better to develop behavioral methods of coping with one's problems than to dissolve them with a pill. This is why self-evaluation and honesty are important ingredients toward the ultimate victory.

RACEHORSES AND TURTLES

Dr. Hans Selye, in Montreal, acknowledged world pioneer of early stress research, has suggested in his books and in several face-to-face interviews with me, that each individual should evaluate his or her own healthy stress level in the environments of life and operate within those levels.

Dr. Selye generally categorizes us as "racehorses" or "turtles" by nature. Everyone knows that a racehorse loves to run and will die if it is corralled and confined, while a turtle will die from exhaustion if forced to run on a treadmill moving too fast for his own, unique, step-by-step nature. Through an honest evaluation of our environment, we also will be able to differentiate between a homicidal maniac and a harmless drunk. In this way, our responses to the environment will be healthy and more effective. The only time we should get upset and pump the adrenaline into the body is in the face of imminent physical danger or to compete successfully in an athletic contest.

JOG YOUR HOSTILITIES AWAY

While expressing emotions such as love, joy, compassion, and exhilaration is healthy and desirable, it may be beneficial to us if we can minimize the overt expression of hostility, anger, depression, loneliness, and anxiety. The only healthy expression of the fight-or-flight emotion is in the face of a life-or-death situation. In most of our daily confrontations, hostility and anger can be dealt with by deep breathing, relaxation, and an exercise program involving gross physical impact such as running, racketball, handball, golf, or tennis.

If we want to conquer undesirable emotional responses in ourselves, we must learn to go through the outward movements of the desirable, positive dispositions that we prefer to cultivate. By anticipating the actions of others through empathy and by remaining open and flexible, we will not allow others to ruin our days with their bad days or to rain on our parade.

PROBLEMS ARE NORMAL (ASK THE GREAT BARRIER REEF!)

One of the best ways to properly evaluate and adapt to the many environmental stresses of life is to simply view them as normal.

Earl Nightingale recently told me of his visit, with his son, to the Great Barrier Reef, which stretches 1,800 miles from New Guinea to Australia. He noticed that the coral polyps on the inside of the reef, where the sea was tranquil and quiet in the lagoon, appeared pale and lifeless, while the coral on the outside of the reef, subjected to the surge of the tide and the power of the waves, were bright and vibrant, with splendid colors and flowing growth. Earl asked his guide why this was so. "It's very simple," came the reply. "The coral on the lagoon side dies rapidly, with no challenge for growth and survival, while the coral facing the surge and power of the open sea, thrives and multiplies because it is challenged and tested everyday. And so it is with every living organism on earth." The adversity and failures in our lives, if adapted to and viewed as normal corrective feedback to use to get back on target, serve to develop in us an immunity against anxiety, depression, and the adverse responses to stress.

FROM BIRTH TO DEATH, WITH THE LEAST NUMBER OF OVERHAULS

Now that we honestly understand that there is more abundance in the environment than we could ever get in a thousand lifetimes, and that we have been viewing our environment with a negative eye, we are ready to move inward into our own internal lifestyle. Our next step is to develop an attitude toward our physical self-honesty.

How's your body these days? Are you fat and sluggish? Are you gaunt and nervous? Do you puff going up a flight of stairs? What kind of fuel do you put in your magnificent machine, your one and only transportation vehicle for life? Is it full of smoke? Are your brain and liver pickled in alcohol? Do you view your body as an old rackety heap parked by the curb to get you from birth to death with the least number of overhauls? Do you think if your battery goes dead, you'll simply get a pacemaker? Or if your carburetor gets clogged, you'll simply get a coronary-artery bypass operation? If you're like me, you probably can't afford to use high-test fuel in your "machine," and you probably stop by Taco Loco and stick a bean burrito in your tank every day for lunch. Do you use high-test meals and nutrition or hit-and-run low-test junk food? In self-evaluating our own bodies, we need to understand that we cannot trade them in for a new model and that their performance in the outside world is largely dependent upon good health. You can only do good if you feel good. And if we abuse our "machine," we won't get to use it as long.

"THE GROCERY BAG OVER THE HEAD CURE"

One of the best ways to develop an attitude of self-honesty about your body is to try an experiment that I did that absolutely blew my mind. I went into my bedroom and locked the door (I thought). I listened for footsteps; there didn't seem to be any. I took off all of my clothes and began the ritual of examining myself nude in front of a full-length mirror. But before I actually looked at myself in this condition, I gave myself some honest self-evaluation. I stuck a paper grocery bag over my head, with eyeholes cut out, and then gazed intently at the "new" me. With a paper sack over my well-known face, I became a stranger in the nude. I broke out into uncontrollable, raucous laughter. I was staring at the "Incredible Hulk" with a paper bag over his head. I turned to the side and gave myself a side view and stopped laughing. I did another turn and got a look at the rear-view mirror. I wheeled around and said, "I don't know who you are, but I wish you'd get dressed and get out."

As I stood there in complete astonishment, viewing the flabby stranger with a bag over his head, my wife walked in unannounced. As her mouth fell open and her eyes widened, I quickly recovered my composure and made the only comment that could be acceptable under such circumstances. I blurted out, "Trick or treat, dear." She took one objective look at the "new" me from the chin down and said, "I'll take the trick." She said, "If you are going to expose yourself like that and play these silly games, why not be kind to yourself and when you stick the bag over your head, don't cut eye-holes out. You'll like what you see a lot better."

When you look in the mirror day after day, your friendly face is used to seeing yourself and has rationalized all of your flaws, even the flab and dark circles. Put the paper sack over that familiar face. It's an experience you'll remember for weeks to come.

A PARTS INVENTORY FOR YOUR "FERRARI"

Now that you've gotten a good look at yourself as others see you, you can begin to take the next steps rapidly. Go to the medicine cabinet and take a look at all the pills and beauty aids that are getting you by and helping you rationalize your current condition. Go to the refrigerator and take an inventory of the kind of food that you are storing for your everyday use to power that magnificent Apollo spacecraft or the Ferrari that you are tweaking and tuning, as your body, to win the Grand Prix or Le Mans, on a daily basis. Check the freezer, look in the cupboards, look in your clothes closet, check your dresser drawers, take a good look at your garage, look in the trunk and in the glove compartment of your car. Take a good look at your physical world and see what your approach has been.

To properly evaluate your physical world, schedule a comprehensive physical at least every two years with your own physician or a reputable clinic. Since you and I frequently blow $500 on the tables and slot machines in Las Vegas, why not invest a similar amount in evaluating your own body. Not just a blood pressure and urine test, a "thank-you" exam. Instead, every two years schedule an appointment at a Mayo or Scripps Clinic or with your physician for an even more detailed physical. Get the works: blood work, EKG, upper and lower GI series, X-rays, eyes, etc. Don't wait for the flat tire, engine knock, or dead battery. Get a prevention check and a tune-up. Make that appointment for a teeth-cleaning session you've been putting off and start using the dental floss that's been sitting in your medicine cabinet.

IT'S ALL IN MY HEAD!

The next and most critical area of honesty to address ourselves to is to ask ourselves the question: Where am I coming from mentally? Since it is our attitude toward our body that makes us want to improve our physical fitness, and since our body is the magnificent machine that flies us throughout the environment, the most important consideration of all in self-honesty as the first element in the Winner's Edge is: What is my mental outlook toward myself in life? Have I been selling myself short, or have I been overconfident in my abilities.

THE GREAT AMERICAN COP-OUT

In my opinion, the current self-awareness movement is an American cop-out. We're so bored with our own abundance in this country that we're using the self-awareness fads to make us feel like we're accomplishing something. We can hardly wait to get on the newest bandwagon for the latest cult in our never-ending search for something else. In America, you're not "in," if you're not into one of the new so-called enlightenment movements of some kind.

The pursuit of mind-expanding techniques toward a heightened state of awareness has been a mysterious journey beginning, perhaps, in the high mountains of Tibet. Today, the quest for mental and physical self-awareness ranges from the ridiculous to the sublime: from electronic hi-fi stereos and alpha brain-wave simulators to hashish; from LSD trips to Scientology; from pyramid power to est; from primal scream to horoscopes; from "Moonies" to biorhythms and the quiet meditation of Maharishi Mahesh Yogi. The interesting point about all these courses, seminars, and mind-expanding guru experiences that we gorge ourselves with as a weekly and monthly diet here in the United States, is that the effects of these may soon wear off and we go back to being ourselves. About the only thing we've usually gained is a little more disillusionment and a little more confusion about the real answers in life.

No wonder there is so much discord in family, social, and international life. Everyone hears a different drummer, sees through a different lens, perceives through a different filter, and decides as a result of a different computer program in his or her own unique brain. Our constant, restless pursuit for the fleeting butterfly of happiness and the search for something else is the direct result of a feeling of helplessness or a lack of responsibility for managing our own behavior in an effective way. It's also a result of looking at the world through negative eyeglasses; we see the weeds and step on the flowers in the environment. We spend most of our time in the pursuit of diversion rather than in the pursuit of direction. We constantly make the excuse that we just want to find ourselves, and, sure enough, in twenty years we find ourselves twenty years older.

THE MIND CRISIS

The real crises in life are not the crises that occur between countries, not the energy crisis, not the Middle-East crisis, and not a crisis of illness or the crisis of cancer, but the real one is the crisis in our mind. Most of our activities are devoted to tension-relieving rather than goal-achieving projects. Instead of tackling the most important priorities that would make us successful and effective in life, we prefer the path of least resistance and do things simply that will relieve our tension, such as shuffling papers and majoring in minors.

Our mind, seemingly the smallest part of us, is really the largest area of all and controls our actions and reactions in both our environmental and physical arenas. Our attitudes in our mental and spiritual worlds are controlled by the thought processes inside our brain and central nervous systems. Talk about abundance! Dr. William James, a recognized leader in early psychology, said that even the most effective humans utilize less than ten percent of their mental potential. We now know that it is much less than ten percent; perhaps even less than one percent of our mental potential is utilized over our entire life span.

NO LIMITS OTHER THAN SELF-IMPOSED!

The Brain Research Institute at the University of California at Los Angeles has concluded that the ultimate creative capacity of the human brain may be infinite. No limits other than self-imposed! Your brain is a Xerox machine, a Polaroid one-step camera, a Betamax video-tape recorder, a wide-screen Technicolor projector, a thousand IBM computers, plus ten billion miniature microfilm cartridges, all delicately designed in one storage battery, floating in an electrochemical solution.

With this virtually untapped and limitless resource, why aren't we more creative, inventive, and successful? Laziness, to be sure, is one mental block. *Why bother?* Fear is another big block. *It's too risky for me!* And it isn't just fear of failure that holds us back. It's more often *fear of success.* Because we can't see our potential, we're beaten from the start and so we make the excuse, *"It's not worth it to succeed."* But what we're really saying is, *"I'm not worth the effort."* This negative self-esteem, plus a low self-image, resulting from negative attitudes, is the major energy gap preventing the release of full human actualization.

Attitude is the answer. In order to feel good physically and to do good in the outer world, you need to get your head together through constructive thinking, not through superficial lip service, nor through one self-awareness cult after another, but by dedicated learning of new, healthy responses to the stimuli of life. In order to get rid of that mental crisis we are all facing, we need to make that moment of truth that every winner experiences at some time or another in life as the first and most important step in self-development: it is understanding how much potential and abundance we have and how little we have done to challenge our minds. It is realizing that each human being on earth is a person with equal rights to fulfill his or her own potential in life. It is understanding that skin color, birthplace, religious beliefs, sex, financial status, and intelligence, are not measures of worth or worthiness. It is accepting the fact that every human being is a distinctly unique individual—and thinking how good that is. No two people are alike, not even identical twins.

WE'RE NOT ON THE SAME WAVELENGTH!

We are unique in our fingerprints, unique in our footprints, even in our lipprints. Bell Telephone has discovered that each of us speaks with a sound frequency unmatched by any other person, and it is in the process of developing a "voice print" system that will provide instant, positive identification electronically. Before the year 2000, it may be possible to do away with ID cards, credit cards, phone calls to banks, signature comparisons, and fingerprint checks. By stating your name audibly into a microphone at the counter, window, or checkstand, your "voice print" frequency will be compared with the one on file at a central computer. No more phony checks or stolen credit cards. We speak at different frequencies and think at different frequencies.

How many times have you heard people say: "We're not on the same wavelength!" We, in the human race, have been trying to get on the same wavelengths for many centuries. The first step toward gaining the Winner's Edge in life and developing that critical attitude for success is understanding that we must seek and walk with truth every day of our lives and always be open to different alternatives and better ways to win. The foundation upon which every great life has been built includes the cornerstones of truth, integrity, and honesty. They must be present for any real and lasting success of any kind. All we really need to learn, accept, and internalize to begin to be a healthy human being with a positive attitude under every circumstance is to ask ourselves the questions: "Is this true?" "Is this honest?" If we can answer yes, or if we can seek the truth from someone who has experienced it, we can move ahead to action with the solid realization that we have taken care of the cause and that the effect will take care of itself.

THE MOMENT OF TRUTH

Make this moment the moment of truth about yourself. Admit that you have been selling yourself short all of your life. Accept the fact that you have the opportunity to experience more environmental, physical, and mental/spiritual abundance than you could use in a thousand lifetimes. Open up your lenses to the possibilities and alternatives available in your life.

Instead of biorhythm computers, astrological signs, gurus, cults, and the federal government, you take credit for determining, creating, and making your own place in this world. You are in the driver's seat in your own life. In many respects, you've exerted control since you were born and cried for milk and a dry diaper. You can learn how to respond and adapt more successfully to the stresses of life by accepting responsibility today for causing your own effects. You alone hold the key to your reactions to people who want to rain on your parade. Remember, it's not so much what happens that counts in life—it's how you take it. The real essence of awareness is that everything in life is volitional and that each of us has many more choices and alternatives than we are willing to consider.

A change in your attitude will bring a change in your lifestyle and your many environments will change automatically. Begin to appreciate and understand your own uniqueness. Also, appreciate the difference in others. Relax and learn how to respond positively to stress. Change for the better that which can be changed. Remove from your presence those negative influences that cannot be changed. Adapt and adjust to those negative influences that cannot be changed or removed.

SELF-HONESTY ACTION REMINDERS

Here are some action reminders to help you develop more self-honesty as an element of your critical attitude for success:

1. *Take the blame and credit* for your position in life honestly and openly.
2. *Be more curious* about everything in your world. Observe the wonder and abundance in nature. Stop feeling sorry for yourself. If you are alive and enjoy some degree of health, you've got it made. Read book digests so that you can share all of the best sellers, as well as read a good book a month. Listen to audio cassettes. Take your librarian to lunch. Seek out and gain counsel from the most successful people in your profession and hobbies.
3. *Break the daily and weekly routine* you have set. Get out of that comfortable rut. Unplug the TV for a month. Get to work via a different route or via another mode of transportation. Take the kids to a symphony or a puppet show. Plan a skiing trip to Chile or New Zealand on the Fourth of July. Have your children give one of their best toys to an orphan this Christmas. If you take showers, take a bath for a change. Instead of taking a Valium, take a walk near the flowers and trees.
4. *Look at yourself honestly* through other people's eyes. Imagine being your parents. Imagine being that person

married to you. Imagine being your child. When you walk into a room or office, imagine that each person is thinking two descriptive adjectives about you, such as "well-dressed, confident" or "aloof and nervous." What would the adjectives about you be in each case? Why?

5. Carry the affirmative motto: *"My rewards in life will reflect my service and contribution,"* with you in every daily transaction.

6. *Be empathic. Learn to feel how others feel* and consider where they are coming from before criticizing. Even if you can't feel *for* everyone you meet, be certain that you feel *with* every living thing you encounter.

7. *Look for truth and speak the truth.* Don't let the ads and the fads make you one of the countless victims of greed and the fringe subcultures. When you read something that impresses you, check the source. When in doubt, call the research department of a national publication you trust or call a major university you respect. If it really works wonders, it will be available everywhere, like aspirin. If it's a breakthrough, look for it to be announced by reputable news authorities and government agencies. Rather than hearing what you want to hear, listen for the facts of the matter. Remember, everything you think is your opinion, based upon your impressions from limited sources. Keep expanding your sources from the best authorities. View everything with a certain open-minded skepticism, to explore it without prejudice, yet skeptical enough to research and test its validity.

8. *Make a self-evaluation list* (two columns) of "I ams." Assets, or "I am good at," in one column; Liabilities, or "I need improvement in," in the other column. Pick your

ten best traits and the ten traits that need most improvement. Take the first three liabilities and schedule an activity or find a winner who will help you improve in each of these three areas. Forget about the rest of the liabilities. Remember, relish, and dwell on all ten of your best assets. They will take you anywhere you want to go in life!

9. *Invest in your own knowledge* and skill development. Since the only real security in life is the kind that is inside each of us, practice what Ben Franklin wrote: "If an individual empties his purse into his head, no one can take it from him." A nearby university usually will offer extension and continuing education programs and the more legitimate ongoing mental and physical fitness programs as well.

10. *Take thirty precious minutes each day for you* alone. Use this extra half hour of your life to wake up and live. Use this time to answer the question: How can I best spend my time today on priorities that are important to me? Be completely aware and honest that your life belongs to you and that all that exists in your life is seen out of your own eyes and experienced by your own mind and body. Turn every mental crisis you are now facing into an opportunity for more personal growth.

▌▌▌
SELF-ESTEEM

SELF-ESTEEM is perhaps the most important and basic element that makes up that critical attitude for success that gives an individual the Winner's Edge in life. It is that deep-down, inside-the-skin feeling of your own worth. "You know, I like myself. I really do like myself. Given my parents and my background, I'm glad I'm me. I'd rather be me than anyone else living or at any other time in history." This the self-talk of a winner, and positive self-talk is the key to developing self-esteem. Winners develop strong beliefs of self-worth and self-confidence. They weren't necessarily born with these good feelings, but as with every other habit, they have learned to like themselves through practice.

STAND BY! THINGS ARE GOING TOO WELL!

It's a wonder that any of us in today's society have managed to reach adulthood with any degree of self-esteem. We already have discussed the tremendous emphasis in society and in the environment on the negative bombardment of our senses with every possible deviant behavior and every possible wrongdoing in life, as if to constantly remind us that things aren't going well in the world. In fact, most of the time when things start going well, we always mention to our friends, "I have a feeling something bad is going to happen, because things are going too well." From the barber shop, to the pool hall, from the beauty parlor, to the grocery store, the chitchat is the same: "Isn't it terrible what is happening in the world?" "Things sure aren't like they used to be." "The world's going to hell."

CORRECTION TO PERFECTION: PLANTING THE WEEDS!

As parents and teachers, we have been as responsible for developing the continued guilt trip that has been passed down through the centuries to our children as any other source or any other medium. I don't know about you, but I've always wanted my children to grow up to be real winners, real competitors in the game of life, and to go for it.

I have six children, and the firstborn always took the brunt of my education in parenthood by trial and error. I was always eager to correct them to perfection. When my children were quiet, nice, and well-behaved, that was normal and natural and for that they got no response. When they misbehaved, or did something wrong, however, I was very quick to correct them and point out what they were doing wrong. Pretty soon, they got the idea that doing something wrong was a good way to get attention from their parents.

As we have passed on inferior feelings to our children, you and I grew up playing an inferior role to the adults in our lives as well. We were told what to do and what not to do. We were constantly reminded of our shortcomings in phrases such as: "Don't interrupt; children should be seen and not heard!" "Big boys don't cry." "Don't you get angry with me; I'll give you something to cry about." I'll never forget my son's fourth birthday party. As soon as he blew out the candles, he reached in and grabbed the biggest piece of cake for himself. I quickly chided him, "Don't be a little pig. It's polite to take the smaller piece!" Why didn't I realize that it was his birthday and he was just trying to feel special for a moment. When my two young daughters crawled all over me while I was watching the evening news on television, and I held them off saying, "Here, don't bother Daddy now, I'm watching Walter Cronkite. I'll play with you after dinner." how could I know that I was rejecting their affection at that moment? And there was the time the kids wanted to show me the country store that they had so proudly built out in the garage during the afternoon. They asked me to come out and play store with them, but I told them that I was watching *Monday Night Football,* and it was a very important last quarter. Why didn't I realize that they just wanted to show me something that they were doing. When I went out to check it, of course it had been put away, and they had gone to bed long before the final gun. And when my children brought home their schoolwork paper with 78 right and 22 wrong, why did I say, "It looks like your paper's got the measles with all those red marks. When you get a 100 or a star, I'll put it up on the refrigerator with a little butterfly magnet."? Other examples: "Don't touch yourself, you're not old enough to do that." "Here, let Dad show you how to do it right." It is little wonder that puberty is being reached so early now and that pregnancy can occur in young females at the age of 10.8 to 11 years old. Children can hardly wait to grow up so that they can do fun and important things like the grown-ups do. They can't wait to get out from being the little stumblebums they think we see them as.

The constant negative bombardment from the environment, from the media, and from our parents and teachers can take its toll, and if practiced continually, can create the troubled teens and the generation gap. Low achievers in life water and cultivate the early seeds of inferior feelings with their imaginations and develop a strong, prickly weed that sticks and irritates them for years to come. As we grow up with these humble feelings, we walk a tight rope between humility, which is a good trait, and humiliation, which is not good. As we grow up into adulthood, we take the child's view with us.

One true indicator of an individual's opinion of himself is the way he can accept a compliment and the way he qualifies himself in advance. In other words, losers constantly lead with their chin, talk themselves down, and lack the ability to accept any value paid by others. It is incredible how low achievers belittle and demean themselves when others try to pay them value.

SELF-ESTEEM

LOSING SELF-TALK: ADVANCE APOLOGIES AND VALUE REJECTION

Here are some examples of this typical type of no-win communication

Praise: "I'd like to congratulate you on a job well done."
Response: "Oh, it was nothing. I was just lucky I guess."
Praise: "Wow, what a great shot you made."
Response: "Yeah, I closed my eyes and swung. I bet I won't do that again."
Praise: "That's a good-looking suit; is it new?"
Response: "Oh, no, I've been thinking of giving it to the Good Will."

I remember one young woman came into one of my seminars, and I looked at her and said, "Are you alone?" She replied, "No, I'm divorced." I said, "Oh, that's too bad; how long have you been divorced?" She said, "Two years now." I responded, "Gee, what a long court case!" And she said, "No, it was completed two years ago. But divorce is a status." I replied, "No, it is an event. It is not something you have to carry with you the rest of your life. You are now single again or unmarried."

Another gentleman came into my seminar and I noticed he was drinking Perrier water, and I said, "Do you really like that stuff?" He said, "No, I'm an alcoholic." So I took off my shoe and put my foot on the table and showed him my in-grown toenail. He said, "Good Lord, man, what are you doing that for?" I said, "Let's get all our faults out on the table up front." I looked at another woman in the audience and said, "Gee, you have beautiful hair." And she said, "Yes, I've got split ends, and I need to go to the beauty parlor." I said, "Is that a new sweater?" She said, "No, it has a moth hole right here." A woman in my last seminar came up to me and I noticed that she had five beautiful, solid-gold, 24-carat strands around her neck. I looked at them admiringly and said, "Gee, what beautiful gold chains you have around your neck." She said, "I wear them to cover up all the little moles I have." A friend of mine came over to my house and I offered him a glass of Scotch. "How about some Chivas Regal," I said. He replied, "Don't waste your good Scotch on me." I said, "I forgot it was just you; here's the Rot Gut for you, pal." I go out for dinner once a week when I'm on the road and get invited over to people's homes in the cities where I am speaking. Invariably, the hostess qualifies her meal as we are ready to sit down to an absolutely delightful meal. Before we can get so much as one bite of the salad or hors d'oeuvres down, she nervously volunteers, "You'll have to excuse the meat tonight; it's a little tough. I didn't have much time to prepare the meal, because I was busy picking up the children. The dessert was an experiment, and it didn't really turn out the way I wanted it to. But next time it will be better," she said. I almost feel like saying, "Well, I'm not coming over again, because it wasn't a five-star dinner tonight. You've had your chance but you blew it, so I'm not coming over any more."

THE SELF-IMAGE LISTENS AND RECORDS

The person with low self-esteem believes that the quality of humility should be pushed over the cliff into humorous humiliation. The devastating fact is that the self-image is always listening and accepts these negative barbs as facts to store as reality.

Current research on the effects of words and images on the functions of the body offers amazing evidence of the power that words spoken at random can have on body functions monitored on bio-feedback equipment. Since thoughts can raise and lower body temperature, secrete hormones, relax muscles and nerve endings, dilate and constrict arteries, and raise and lower pulse rate, it is obvious that we need to control the language we use on ourselves. That's why winners rarely put themselves down in actions or in words. But losers fall into the trap of saying: "I can't"; "I'm a klutz"; and "I'll try, I'm not saying I will, and I'm not saying I won't, but I'll try."

GOLD MEDALS AND HUNCHED SHOULDERS

One of the best examples of the "lead-with-your-chin" and "inability-to-accept-a-compliment" syndromes was demonstrated for me at dinner during my last wedding anniversary.

My wife and I were in Atlanta, at the Midnight Sun Restaurant. Everything was perfect. We were seated in elegant attire, next to the waterfall, resplendent in candlelight, with twenty-one violins playing the anniversary waltz right on cue. The waiters were in full tuxedo. We couldn't help but notice one particular waiter who had been assigned to our table. He was six feet tall, had flashing eyes and straight white teeth, and looked very much like a 28-year-old-version of Omar Sharif. He was a medical student working his way through college, and my wife and I were both impressed with his manner and his looks.

When he came up to take our order, it took him less than 30 seconds to volunteer his complete feelings of his own worthiness to us: "What'll it be, sir?" he asked with a smile. "We'll have the Veal Diane Flambé, prepared at the table," I replied, with a wink. "It's special, it's our anniversary." He gave me a funny look and then volunteered his self-esteem: He stammered, "Ah, 'er, it's my first week on the job, sir, and I don't think I can prepare that flaming Veal Diane at the table. I guess I could get another waiter to help me do it, but I don't think it will turn out very well, and, besides, I might splatter some grease on your wife's dress. May even set it on fire! Why don't you just be good to yourselves and order something relatively simple from the menu, so I won't have to try to prepare it?" I stared at him in disbelief, but I quickly tried to console him, since he was obviously agitated and anxious. "Don't worry about it son," I said. "It's our anniversary tonight, and we're thinking more of each other than we are about the dinner. You can go ahead and experiment on us. We're nice people and fairly easy to get along with. We won't criticize you or pay that much attention. Besides, you'll have to prepare it sooner or later, so you might just as well experiment on us!" He replied, in surprise, "I already told you how it was going to turn out; boy, you're really asking for it!" I assured him to go ahead, "Had you not mentioned it, we wouldn't even have known the difference. We'll have the Veal Diane."

Well, he struggled, and worked, and got assistance from the other waiters. The smoke filled the room, and my wife and I managed to pleasantly chew the small, black, spongy pieces of veal that had been the result of his excruciating efforts. But for those efforts, which were honest, I decided to give him some real value for service rendered (which, incidentally, you and I receive every day from people in the form of compliments or any other remarks they make as a result of what we do for them.) When he brought the check on the silver tray, I paid the bill and laid a thirty-dollar tip right on top. He looked at it and backed away from the value I paid. "But, oh gosh, sir, it wasn't worth that much!" I quickly took twenty-five dollars back and put it in my pocket. He gave me a startled look and said, "Well, it was worth more than five!" I said, "No it wasn't, son. If it wasn't worth it to you, it certainly wasn't worth it to me." He forced a smile and looked up from his feet and said, "Why don't you try me again?" I put a ten-dollar bill back on the tray. He struggled for the words and finally said with a question, "Thank you?" "Kind of heavy, isn't it, the word thank you?" I offered. He said, "Yes, it kind of feels uncomfortable; kind of like a gold medal going around your neck to hunch your shoulders forward." I nodded, "But when you pull them back and just say 'thank you,' it makes you accept the value paid." I laid another ten on the tray. The thank-you came easier this time, and he smiled and his eyes flashed bright. I put down the final five dollars, and he said, "Thank you very much, sir; have a nice evening." I said, "You're welcome, son, and, by the way,

71

don't ever qualify yourself in advance. Never lead with your chin. Always put your best self forward. People will find out all they need to know about you in their own way without you volunteering your shortcomings. And when anyone pays you value in the future, simply say 'thank you.' That is all that is required. Accept the value paid as being earned by you and something that you own.''

THE FAILURE SYNDROME

Scientists have been studying a native tribe in South America who had been dying prematurely from a strange malady for many generations. It was finally discovered that the disease was caused by the bite of an insect, which lives in the walls of their adobe homes. The natives have several possible solutions: they can destroy the insects with an insecticide; they can destroy and rebuild their homes; they can move to another area where there are no such insects; or, they can continue to live and die early, just as they have done for generations. They have chosen to remain as they are and die early, the path of least resistance and no change.

Many people have a similar attitude about personal development. On the one hand, they know that learning brings about change, but on the other hand, they resist change. They know that many people have overcome enormous obstacles to become great, but they can't imagine it happening to them and so they resign themselves to be the also-rans in life, wishing and envying away their lives. These low achievers learn the habit of concentrating on their failures and the negative events in their lives with self-talk that reinforces the losing cycle. Because they are controlled by external standards set by others, they often set their sights too high. Thus, they are unrealistic to begin with and as they fail to reach their goals again and again, these failures become set in their subconscious self-images as targets and goals of their own. This explains why so many people have permanent potential. In other words, why they *almost* succeed over and over, having temporary, fleeting successes, which fail to materialize into a solid lifestyle.

THE BLOWHARDS

It is also interesting to note that the blowhards in life, the ones who yell loudest for service and attention, are really calling for help because of low self-esteem. What they are really shouting is: "Help, look at me, please." It is said that John Dillinger ran into a farm house and repeatedly told the occupants: "My name is John Dillinger. I'm not going to hurt you; I just wanted you to know that my name is Dillinger."

Psychiatrist Bernard Holland has pointed out that although juvenile delinquents appear to be very independent and have a reputation of being braggarts, particularly about how they hate everyone in authority, they protest too loudly. Underneath this hard exterior shell, says Dr. Holland, "is a soft, vulnerable, inner person, who wants to be dependent upon others." However, they cannot get close to anyone, because they will not trust anyone. At some point in the past, they were hurt by a person important to them and they dare not leave themselves open to be hurt again. They must always have their defenses up. To prevent further rejection and pain, they attack first. Thus, they drive away the very people who would love them, if given half a chance, and could help them. This description also applies to many people we associate with who are not juvenile delinquents. They may be professional peers or even loved ones.

SELF-DOUBT: THE MOTHER OF JEALOUSY

Many people we know are hurt terribly by little things we call social slights. It is a well-known psychological fact that the people who become offended the easiest have the lowest self-esteem. It is the person who feels undeserving, doubts his capabilities, and has a poor opinion of himself who becomes jealous at the drop of a hat. Jealousy, which is the scourge of many marriages, is nearly always caused by self-doubt. The person with adequate self-esteem doesn't feel hostile toward others, isn't out to prove anything, can see the facts more clearly, and isn't demanding in his claims on other people.

Bernard Baruch was once asked how he went about arranging the seating of guests for his dinner parties without offending anyone. He replied he solved the problem by simply allowing his guests to seat themselves, choosing where they wished to sit. As he put it, "The people who matter don't mind, and the people who mind don't matter." The principle that Baruch uncovered is true in all walks of life. Those who know who they are need not be defensive, nor do they have to go out of their way to prove anything. Their solid self-esteem is quite enough to get them anywhere they want to go.

WINNERS CAN AFFORD MODESTY

In today's cosmetic society, there is a real need for values when we consider the true meaning of self-esteem. We seem to be taking a good thing, which is doing the best with what we've got, and going overboard with excessive self-adoration and self-indulgence in an attempt to buy the fountain of youth and superficial esteem. We know, of course, that the kind of house, car, clothing, and possessions we show off to the world represent our attempt to tell others who we are. More important than telling others who we are is that our expressed standards of living serve to remind *us* who we are.

In today's world of easy credit, in what some have called "the plastic age" because of the flood of credit cards and the ease with which they can be obtained and used, almost anyone can arrange to display an expensive car or power boat or motor home in front of his house. Therefore, the tendency to show off many toys and trappings of affluence and material success is more likely to say to others that we are really lacking in self-esteem or self-worth than the fact that we can afford it.

It is fair to say that only an individual who has a strong sense of self-respect or self-esteem can afford to project a modest image to the community. In other words, winners can project success without flaunting it. Winners may not always be able to afford to buy the most expensive things, but they always do the very best with what they can afford.

75

HOW TO DEVELOP SELF-ESTEEM

The word esteem literally means appreciate the value of. Why do we stand in awe of the power and immensity of the sea, the uniqueness of a solar eclipse, the beauty of a flower, a giant redwood, or a sunset, and at the same time, downgrade ourselves? Didn't the same Creator make us? Are we not the most marvelous creation of all, able to think, experience, change our environment, and, more importantly, aren't we able to love? In other words, don't downgrade the product just because you haven't used it properly and effectively to date.

It would be impossible to love another person without first feeling love for yourself, because how could you give away something that you don't have? It is important to develop the deep-down, inside-the-skin feeling of deserving the abundance. Self-esteem is felt even though you may not have done anything yet, but just feel the capability for it.

WINNERS REINFORCE PAST SUCCESSES

Confidence is built on the experience of success. When we begin anything new, we usually have little confidence because we have not learned from experience that we can succeed. This is true when learning to ride a bicycle, ski, figure skate, fly a high-performance jet aircraft, or lead people. It is true that success breeds success. Winners focus on past successes and forget past failures. They use errors and mistakes as a way to learning, then they dismiss them from their minds.

Yet, what do many of us do? We destroy our self-confidence by remembering past failures and forgetting all about our past successes. We not only remember failures, we etch them in our mind with emotion. We condemn ourselves. Winners know it doesn't matter how many times they have failed in the past. What matters is their successes, which should be remembered, reinforced and dwelt upon. To establish true self-esteem, we must concentrate on our successes and look at the failures and negatives in our lives only as corrective feedback to get us on target again. The child's view must be recognized as just that; as serving a purpose in early years, but dropping aside as we mature. Instead of comparing ourselves to others, we should view ourselves in terms of our own abilities, interests, and goals.

THE CRITICAL FIRST IMPRESSION

We can begin by making a conscious effort to upgrade our lifestyle and pay more attention to personal appearance and personal habits. Winners display a simple, radiating charm. They project that warm glow that comes from the inside outwards. Most importantly, self-esteem is transmitted with a smile, which is the universal language that opens doors, melts defenses, and saves a thousand words. A smile is the light in your window that tells others there is a caring, sharing person inside.

Winners are aware that first impressions are powerful and

create lasting attitudes. They understand that interpersonal relationships and professional relationships can be won or lost in about the first four minutes of conversation. They have learned through experience that fairly or unfairly people project and respond to a visceral- or gut-level feeling, which is nearly instantaneous.

We need to respect the fact that we as people usually project on the outside how we really feel about ourselves on the inside. For example, when we aren't feeling well physically, we don't look well on the skin or surface level. And, correspondingly, when we don't feel good about ourselves emotionally or mentally, we don't seem to make a very good impression with our looks, personal grooming, and clothing habits. A recent Harvard study has pointed out that people who feel unattractive, as judged by themselves and their peers, tend to suffer from feelings of loneliness, rejection, and isolation. Schoolchildren who look good are actually treated better, not only by their classmates but by their teachers as well. The term good-looking as we are using it, does not necessarily mean beautiful or handsome like a movie star. Other studies have shown that some of the most beautiful people, physically, are less satisfied, less well-adjusted, and less happy in later life.

SELF-ACCEPTANCE: TO THINE OWN SELF BE TRUE

What can we learn from these insights? Firstly, while we have no choice over the genes we have inherited and thus are stuck with our general shape, structure, and skin, it is to our advantage to take care of our health and appearance and to do what we can to enhance what we've got. Like it or not, we will usually be instantly judged by our looks, which leave a lasting impression. Secondly, since we behave in accordance with the way we think we look, rather than the way we actually look to others, those of us who can learn to be fairly satisfied with our features are way ahead of the game as far as being real winners in life.

Although we are always seeking improvement, the real Winner's Edge in self-esteem is reached when the individual can accept himself or herself just as he or she is at this moment. Since the perfect human has not been discovered, we all need to live with our hang-ups and idiosyncracies—until they can be ironed out.

One of the most important aspects of self-esteem that accounts for successful, dynamic living is that of self-acceptance: the willingness to be one's self and live one's life as it is unfolding, accepting all responsibility for the ultimate outcome. Shakespeare explained it in *Hamlet,* when he has Polonius say: "And this above all, to thine own self be true and it must follow as the night the day/-thou can'st not then be false to any man." To develop and maintain self-esteem as we are right now, we need to find pleasure and pride in our current profession, rather than looking for greener pastures elsewhere. This is the philosophy of mining your "acres of diamonds" right now, right where you are, making changes in your internal reactions rather than searching for external stimulation in a new environment.

RATIONAL DECISIONS AND EMOTIONAL REACTIONS

We also need to base more of our actions and decisions on rational thinking rather than on emotions. Emotions are automatic subconscious reactions. To respond to the daily experiences and challenges of life by reacting only emotionally is to nullify the wisdom and power of the rational mind.

Winners are able to enjoy their emotions, like children probing the depths of love, excitement, joy, and compassion, but they make the decisions that shape their lives through logic and common sense. Marriages today would be much stronger if they were entered into intelligently, as well as emotionally. Except during emergencies, winners usually make important decisions when the adrenalin flow is back to normal.

POSITIVE SELF-TALK IS THE KEY

Perhaps the most important key to the permanent enhancement of self-esteem in the practice of positive self-talk. Every waking moment we must feed our self-images positive thoughts about ourselves and our performances, so relentlessly and vividly that our self-images are in time molded and modified to conform to new, higher standards.

As winners, we need to use constructive feedback and self-talk every day: "I can"; "I look forward to"; "I want to"; "Next time I'll get it right"; "This is what I'll do";

SELF-ESTEEM

"I'm feeling better." As winners we will also accept compliments by simply saying, "Thank You." Bob Hope says thank you. Frank Borman says thank you. Steve Cauthen, after winning the triple crown, doesn't say, "Gee I almost fell off my horse." He says, "Thank you." Can you imagine Neil Armstrong on his return from the moon and you and I run down to Houston to greet him on his return, and he's standing there kicking the dirt. We say, "Congratulations, Neil. "One giant step for mankind!" He replies, "We just got lucky. Who would think you could get half a million miles up and back in something built by the lowest bidder?" No, Neil Armstrong says, "Thank you." So does Jack Nicklaus, Tom Watson, Nancy Lopez, Margaret Thatcher, and every other winner in life. Self-esteem is the quality of simply saying, thank you, and accepting value that is paid to you by others.

Almost without exception, the real winner, whether we speak of sports, business, or any other activity of life, has accepted his own uniqueness, feels comfortable with his image, and is willing to let others know and accept him just as he is. And it is an interesting fact that such a person naturally attracts friends and supporters. He or she seldom has to stand alone. Winners know that contrary to popular belief this feeling of self-acceptance and deserving is not necessarily a legacy from wise and loving parents. History is full of saints who rose from the gutters and literal monsters who grew up in loving families. Recognizing their own uniqueness, they develop and maintain their own high standards.

SELF-ESTEEM: THE DOOR TO HAPPINESS

Accept yourself as you are right now: an imperfect, changing, growing, and worthwhile person. Realize that liking yourself and feeling that you are a super individual in your own special way is not necessarily egotistical. In addition to taking pride in what you are accomplishing, even more importantly enjoy the unique person that you are just by being alive right now. Understand the truth that although we as individuals are not born with equal physical and mental attributes, we are born with equal rights to feel the excitement and joy in believing that we deserve the very best in life. Most successful people believe in their own worth, even when they have nothing but a dream to hold on to. Perhaps more than any other quality, healthy self-esteem is the door to high achievement and happiness. It is one of the most critical elements in that attitude that makes up the Winner's Edge.

SELF-ESTEEM ACTION REMINDERS

Here are some action reminders to help you develop more of the attitude of self-esteem:

1. *Dress and look your best* at all times, regardless of the pressure from your friends and peers. Personal grooming and appearance provide an instantaneous projection on the surface of how you feel inside about yourself.
2. *Take inventory of your good reasons* for self-esteem

today. Write down what your "bag" is; blessings, who and what you are thankful for; accomplishments, what you have done that you are proud of so far; goals, what your dreams and ambitions are.

3. *Set your own internal standards* rather than comparing yourself to others. Accept yourself as you are right now, but keep upgrading your own standards, lifestyle, behavior, professional accomplishments, and relationships by associating with winners.

4. *Volunteer your own name first* in every telephone call and whenever you meet someone new. By paying value to your own name in communication, you are developing the habit of paying value to yourself as an individual.

5. *Respond with a simple, courteous "thank you"* when anyone pays you a compliment for any reason.

6. *Use encouraging affirmative language* when you talk to yourself and to others about yourself. Focus on uplifting and building adjectives and adverbs. Everything you say about yourself is being recorded subconsciously by others and more importantly by your own self-image.

7. *Sit down and create your best horoscope* on paper. List positive alternatives to habits that you seriously want to change. Seek out authorities with proven records of success after whom to model your winning habits.

8. *Look at people in the eyes.* When you speak to anyone for any reason, concentrate on direct eye contact. It is one of the most important nonverbal indicators of self-confidence.

9. *Keep a self-development plan ongoing* at all times. Sketch it out on paper: the knowledge you'll require, the behav-

ior modification you'll achieve, the changes in your life that will result.

10. *SMILE!* In every language, in every culture, it is the light in your window that tells people that there's a caring, sharing individual inside, and it's the universal code for "I'm okay, and you're super, too!"

IV
SELF-IMAGE

A creative self-image is the key to developing that critical attitude for success known as the Winner's Edge. Individuals behave, not in accordance with reality, but with their perception of reality. How the individual feels about himself or herself is everything, for all that he or she ever does or aspires to do will be predicated on that all important concept that is the self-image.

Whether we realize it or not, each of us carries around with us in our mind a videotape cassette, a very complicated video cassette containing (by the time we're 30 years old) some three trillion pictures of ourselves. This videotape may be vague and ill-defined to our conscious awareness. In fact, it may not be consciously recognizable at all. But it is there, complete to the last detail. This self-image is our own conception of the "sort of person I am." It has been built by our own beliefs about ourselves.

Most of these beliefs about ourselves have unconsciously been formed from our past experiences, our successes and failures, our humiliations, our triumphs, and the way other people have reacted to us, especially in early childhood. From all these we mentally construct a "self," or a "video-tape of a self." Once an idea or belief about ourself goes into this picture, it becomes true as far as we, personally, are concerned. We do not question its validity, but proceed to act upon it just as if it were true. Each of us, from childhood on, weaves our own intricate web of self-images out of notions, out of comments from our parents, and environmental training from our teachers and friends. First as offhanded notions, like flimsy cobwebs, then with practice, they become cables to strengthen or shackle our lives.

ARE BLUE EYES BRIGHTER?

Children's self-images are very pliable and susceptible to external guidance and criticism. Young students who are treated as though they are mentally slow by teachers and parents will assume that they are, indeed, inferior to normal children.

You may recall the highly publicized recent experiment conducted by a young primary-grade schoolteacher upon her pupils. With approval from their parents, she told her class that "recent scientific reports had verified that children with blue eyes have greater natural learning abilities than children with brown eyes." She had them make up little signs designating themselves as "blue eyes" or "brown eyes," which were then hung around their necks. After a week or so, the achievement level of the brown-eyed group fell measurably, while the performance of the blue-eyed section improved significantly. She then made a startling announcement to the class. She had made a mistake! It was the blue or lighter eyed people who were the weaker students and the brown or darker eyed ones who were stronger students. She told the class that all babies are born with weak or blue eyes and, as they grow stronger or older, they become brown or dark. Up went the image and achievement of the brown-eyed group. Down came the performance of the blue-eyed children.

WHAT YOU SEE IS WHAT YOU GET!

The student who sees himself as an "F" student or one who is dumb in mathematics will invariably find that his report card bears him out. He then has "proof." A young girl who has an image of herself as the sort of person nobody likes will find indeed that she is avoided at the school dance. She literally invites rejection. Her self-conscious expression, her overanxiousness to please, or perhaps her unconscious hostility toward those she anticipates will affront her, all act to drive away those whom she would attract. In the same manner, a salesman or businessman will find that his actual experiences tend to "prove" his self-image is correct. Because of this objective "proof," it very seldom occurs to a person that his trouble lies in the self-image or in his own evaluation of himself.

THE WINNER'S EDGE

MAXWELL MALTZ'S MAGIC WAND

The late Dr. Maxwell Maltz, plastic surgeon and author of the longtime best seller, *Psycho-Cybernetics,* said that "the most important psychological discovery of this century is the discovery of the self-image." Dr. Maltz may well have been right. There would, at first, appear to be little connection between surgery and psychology. Yet, it was the work of the plastic surgeon and, in particular Dr. Maltz, that first hinted at the real important psychological knowledge. Some thirty years ago, Dr. Maltz reported in his book, *New Faces, New Futures,* of case histories that literally amazed him when dramatic and sudden changes in character and personality resulted when a facial defect was corrected. Changing the physical images in many instances appeared to create an entirely new person. In case after case, the scalpel that he held in his hand became to him a magic wand that not only transformed the patient's appearance, but transformed their whole life. The shy and retiring became bold and courageous. The retarded, stupid boy changed into an alert, bright youngster who went on to become an executive with a prominent firm. The salesman who had lost his touch and his faith in himself, became a model of self-confidence.

I STILL FEEL UGLY!

Strangely enough, Dr. Maltz and other plastic surgeons learned as much, if not more, from their failures as from their successes. It was easy to explain the successes. The boy with the too big ears, who had been told that he looked like a taxi with both doors open, had been ridiculed all his life. Why shouldn't he avoid social contacts? Why shouldn't he become afraid of people and retire into himself? When his ears were corrected, it would seem only natural that the cause of his embarrassment and humiliation had been removed and that he should assume a normal role in his life which he did.

But what about the exceptions that didn't change? The woman who all her life had been terribly shy and self-conscious because of a great big hump in her nose? Although surgery gave her a classic nose and a face that was truly beautiful, she still continued to act the part of the ugly duckling, the unwanted sister who could never bring herself to look another human being in the eye. If the scalpel itself was magic, why did it not work on this woman? And, what about all the others who acquired new faces, but went right on wearing the same old personality? How could the doctors explain the reaction of those people who insisted that surgery had made no difference whatsoever in their appearance? Every plastic surgeon has had this experience and has probably been as baffled as Dr. Maltz. No matter how drastic the change in appearance may be, there are certain patients and people who will insist that "I look just the same as before; you didn't do a thing." Friends, even mates, may scarcely recognize them, may become enthusiastic over their newly acquired beauty, yet the patient herself insists that she can see only slight or no improvement, or in fact deny that any change at all has been made. Comparison of before-and-after photographs does little good except possibly to arouse hostility. By some strange mental block, the patient will rationalize, "Of course, I can see the hump is no longer in my nose, but my nose still looks just the same," or "The scar may not show anymore, but I still feel ugly."

BEAUTY IS IN THE EYES OF THE BEHOLDER

Another clue in the search for the illusive self-image is that not all scars or disfigurements bring shame and humiliation. Consider the fact that Moshe Dayan, the dynamic hero of Israel, wears a patch over his eye to cover up the war disfigurement as proudly as one of us might wear the Medal of Honor.

Persons with normal or very acceptable looks should be free from all psychological handicaps. They should be cheerful, happy, self-confident, and free from anxiety and worry. We know only too well this is not true. As we become an even more cosmetically-based society, in search of narcissistic pleasure and indulgence, there is an increasing stampede of people who visit the office of a plastic surgeon and demand a facelift to cure a purely imaginary ugliness. There are the 35- or 45-year-old women who are convinced that they look old, even though their appearance is perfectly normal and, in many cases, unusually attractive. There are the young girls who are convinced that they are ugly merely because their mouth, nose, or bust measurement does not exactly match that of the currently reigning box-office star. There are men who believe their ears are too big or their noses are too long. No ethical plastic surgeon would even consider operating on these people. But, unfortunately, the quacks or so-called beauty doctors, whom no medical association will admit to membership, have no such qualms. My mother remembers in the 1920's when many women felt ashamed of themselves because they had large breasts. The boyish figure was in vogue and bosoms were taboo. Today, many young girls develop anxieties because they do not have 40-inch busts. In the 1920's, women used to come to Dr. Maxwell Maltz and say, "Make me somebody by reducing the size of my breasts." Today, the plea to plastic surgeons is, "Make me somebody by increasing the size of my breasts." This seeking of identity, this desire for self-hood, this urge to be somebody, is universal.

WE MUST LIVE WITHIN THE LIMITS WE SET!

But we make a mistake when we seek it in conformity to external standards, in the approval of other people, or in material things. You are a unique gift of creation. And what you do with yourself is almost entirely based upon your imagination of your possibilities.

While self-esteem is a general deep-down, inside-the-skin feeling of worthiness, the self-image is very specific. Each of us, male and female, has developed a self-image concerning every talent, every characteristic, and every performance. "I'm a lousy cook; I can't boil an egg." "I'm a good dancer." "I have a great sense of humor." "I have a terrible memory." "I'm a sensitive, warm person." "I'm never on time." "A woman's place is in the home." "I'm a true Leo." "I'm a born loser." Each of us is controlled by these mental pictures we

91

have formed of ourselves. We cannot outgrow these limits we place on ourselves, we can only set new limits within which we must live.

Just as with the stronger and weaker students, there is the image of the stronger and weaker sex. The male-versus-female syndrome. The woman's role in society used to be dominantly shaped by a restricted self-image as a result of associations with the "weaker sex" attitude and with lower, slower and fewer potentials. Today, the emergence of women in society is a major sociological movement. So-called "women's liberation" should be more appropriately labeled "women's elevation." As the self-image of women is elevated, up goes behavior and achievement, down come the self-imposed and outer-imposed barriers, and out come the new opportunities for expression.

IMAGINATION RULES OUR WORLD

Every living organism has a built-in guidance system to help it achieve its goal, which is, in very general terms, to live. In the more primary forms, the goal to live simply means physical survival for both the individual and the species. The built-in mechanism or instinct in animals is limited to finding food and shelter, avoiding or overcoming enemies, and procreation to ensure the survival of the species. In the human being, the goal to live means much more than mere survival. Humans have certain emotional and spiritual needs, which animals do not have.

We often overlook the fact that human beings have a success instinct much more marvelous and much more complex than that of any animal. Animals cannot select their goals; their goals are preset. Their success mechanism is limited to those inborn, goal images which are called instincts. The success instinct in the human being, however, has something that animals will never possess and this is creative imagination. Thus, the human being of all creatures is more than a creature. He or she is also a creator. The human being is the only creature on the earth that can direct his or her success mechanism by the use of the creative imagination, or imaging ability. Napoleon said, "Imagination rules the world." Einstein put it more simply: "Imagination is the world." The way you picture your world, the way you perceive it, is the world in which you live.

THE SELF-IMAGE: OUR AUTOMATIC PILOT

The imagination we hold of our self, or our self-image, determines the kind and scope of person we are. It is our "life-controlling mechanism." Our self-image dwells at the subconscious level of thinking. Although the term "subconscious mind" is used loosely by laymen, it is probably more accurate to think of it not as a mind but rather as a mechanism or an ability of the mind.

Our self-image can be compared to a guidance computer or automatic pilot. Guidance computers are devices which can be programmed to seek an image or target. They are installed in projectiles like the homing torpedo and the ballistic missile, which are then guided by these highly sophisticated electronic systems that seek the target unerringly,

93

through the use of electronic-data feedback. The human brain operates similarly, but is far more marvelous and complex than any system man could ever invent. With the homing torpedo, you set your target and this self-activated system, constantly monitoring feedback signals from the target area and adjusting the course setting in its own navigational guidance computer, makes every correction necessary to stay on target and score a hit. Programmed incompletely, non-specifically, or aimed at a target too far out of range, the homing torpedo will wander erratically until its propulsion system fails or it self-destructs. So it is with each individual human system in life. Set a goal or an image and this self-motivated system, constantly monitoring self-talk and environmental feedback about the goal and adjusting the self-image settings in its subconscious creative achievement mechanism, makes every decision necessary to reach the goal.

Information fed into your subconscious memory bank stays there. The billions of separate items of input over a lifetime are all there waiting retrieval. They can never willfully be erased by you. They can be overridden or modified, but you are stuck with them for life. For example, brain surgery by world authorities, Dr. Penfield and Dr. Rogers at the Montreal Neurological Institute, strongly supports this premise—literally confirms it as a fact. In their research, when brain cells were stimulated with an electrode, patients reported the sensation of reliving scenes from the past. The recall was so vivid that all details were present, including sounds, colors, tastes, and odors. The patients were not just remembering, but reliving the experiences as if they were happening again.

SELF-IMAGE = ATTITUDE = SUCCESS

During every moment of our lives, we program our self-image to work for us or against us. Since it is only a mechanism, having no judging function, it strives to meet the objectives and goals we set for it regardless of whether they are positive or negative, true or false, right or wrong, safe or dangerous. Its sole function is to follow instructions, implicitly, based upon previous inputs, like a computer reading its tape and responding automatically.

Scientists agree that the human nervous system cannot tell the difference between an actual experience and an experience imagined vividly, emotionally and in detail. This is why attitude determines success. Because attitude is an imagined inclination toward the achievement of a certain event. Therefore, attitude is everything since the human system cannot tell the difference between an actual performed experience and an imagined synthetic experience. Many of your everyday decisions are based upon information about yourself that has been stored as truth, but is just a figment of your own imagination, shaded by your environment.

THE TENACIOUS, TIME-GROWN SELF-IMAGE

The Winner's Edge—as it applies to the self-image—is understanding the tenacity of the time-grown self-image and realizing that it takes days and weeks of constant "imagineering" and simulation to modify or put new inputs on top of the old programs.

An overt illustration of this tenacity of the time-grown, self-image (similar to plastic surgery where the patient doesn't see any change because they've been feeling ugly for twenty-one years) is in the study of amputees. At Walter Reed Hospital, after the Vietnam War, I had the opportunity to observe and study the adjustment period that amputees went through to return into society. In reality—physically, consciously, at the judgment level of thinking—the limb is gone. But for several weeks, sometimes longer, the patient will experience pain, itching, or tingling in hands or feet that are no longer there. During the night, some try to get out of bed and walk, only realizing after they have fallen, that they are legless! The self-image lingers on, long after reality has changed. If it requires several weeks to mentally accept a new self-image brought about by a permanent physical change, then consider the self-discipline, persistence, and dedication required to change your image or reality totally from the inside.

WINNERS PRACTICE ON AND OFF THE PLAYING FIELD

The Winner's Edge is telling yourself over and over again with words, pictures, concepts, and emotions that you are winning each important personal victory *now.* Winners practice on and off their playing field in life, including in and out of the office and in and out of the home. They create in their imagination or simulate each experience they want. Every winner I've ever met in every walk of life, male or female, uses the technique of mental simulation every day to modify his or her own self-image. I met a world-champion Russian figure skater and she said, "I rarely fall because I practice each sequence in my imagination at night with my eyes closed and could successfully perform my routine blindfolded with no hesitation." I sat next to a gentleman on a recent flight to Chicago who was making a weird, high-pitched humming sound with his eyes closed. I turned the overhead air nozzle on his face and asked him if he wanted me to call the stewardess to come to his aid. He retorted indignantly, "I beg your pardon, I'm an oboeist for the Chicago Symphony Orchestra and I'm practicing for tonight's performance. Now if you'll excuse me . . . "

Did you ever see former Olympic champion highjumper Dick Fosbury do the famous "Fosbury Flop," a backward swan dive over a seven-foot three-inch bar? I observed him firsthand in Mexico City at the Olympic Games more than a decade ago and noticed that he rocked back and forth for several minutes with his eyes closed before charging straight ahead for his backward leap. Dick Fosbury "saw" himself successfully going over the bar in his imagination while rocking back and forth before each jump. French skier John Claude Killy won the giant slalom in his imagination first. Mental simulation or imagination is an excellent way to practice skiing and gain confidence. Feet together, weight properly balanced, correct knee position, down the fall line, watch for mogules, feel the pure, crisp snow, the wind, the speed, the exhilaration of doing it all yourself. But you are not doing this on the hill. Now you are back in your warm chalet, in front of a fire, with some hot, buttered rum. You're simulating in preparation for tomorrow. For champions, it is the Winner's Edge. For beginners, it is a great way to conquer fear. After all, in your imagination, you never fall!

GETTING UP TO OR BACK TO WHERE YOU BELONG

Any permanent change in your personality or behavior should first involve a change in your self-image, reinforced by a change in lifestyle. Then your long-range behavior performance will automatically follow. Your behavior, personality, or achievement level is usually consistent with your self-image. A golfer's handicap makes a good illustration. You see yourself after so many rounds as a lifetime 18 handicap. You shoot consistently in the 90s. One day you don't pay much attention to yourself and shoot a fantastic 36, or par, on the front nine. That's not like you. You're playing over your head. Considering your known handicap, and your self-image as a golfer, what do you do on the back nine? Right! You adjust with a tree, water, and sand-seeking ball. You get back to being "yourself." The tension finally goes away with a comfortable 55 on the back nine. Just about right on your self-image handicap.

What could an undernourished Black youth on the streets of San Francisco imagine, especially since he was suffering from a crippling disease associated with malnutrition called rickets, which made his legs weak and slightly bowed? He was given encouragement and leg braces. Not much of a head start in life. Yet, this kid with the funny legs and the funny first name somehow developed a creative preview of coming attractions. When he was eleven years old, he attended a banquet honoring the legendary National Football League running back, Jim Brown. "I'll break every record you set," the youngster promised Brown. This kid has since shortened his funny first name, because his name is seen and used so much today. You may not remember little Orenthal, but you certainly do recognize the great O. J. Simpson, having set rushing records and now running through airports while renting cars on TV—running—all the way to the bank and into sports history.

Was it foolish to imagine and dream of being the first woman president? Golda Meir didn't think so. Although, who would have foreseen that a middle-class old grandma, who had divorced her husband, who could have been selling lox and bagels in New York, could have gone on to become one of the most dramatic, inspirational, and intelligent leaders in the world.

THE WINNER'S EDGE IS SIMULATING WINNING

Neil Armstrong's vision began as a lad. In an interview immediately following his historic first step on the moon, he said, "Ever since I was a little boy, I dreamed I would do something important in aviation." It is fascinating that the dreams, daydreams, and imagination of a child can shape a destiny so dramatically that this particular youth was to grow up to make the most significant footprints on the sands of time of any aviator during the first century of man's flight. Here again, the Winner's Edge separates the pipe dreams, the daydreams, the wishy-washy, Walter Mitty concepts from the real achievement dreams.

However, it's not enough to have a dream or to see yourself do some amazing feat. We spend most of our time practicing or imagining our bad habits, rather than our good ones, or even looking for good ones. We are relentless in our expertise at becoming accomplished losers. The Winner's Edge is simulating winning. Winners practice as if they are first, even if their challenge is a first for mankind.

Astronauts are living examples of taking this Winner's Edge to its proper point of completion. I devoted a year of my life studying, interviewing, and working with the Apollo crews, playing "let's pretend we're going to the moon." No one had ever done it before. Who, other than Jules Verne, Ray Bradbury or Isaac Asimov really dreamed it possible? The astronauts became masters at mental simulation. They practiced bobbing up and down in a rubber raft at sea, responding to the feeling of weightlessness to be experienced in outer space. They practiced day after day in the desert with a simulated lunar-excursion module as if they were really landing it on the surface of the moon. Hour after hour, month after month, year after year, they memorized and simulated the exact theoretical, imagined steps with hundreds of critically vital sequences that NASA scientists had imagined would take them safely to the moon and back. Then Neil Armstrong took the first giant step and transmitted his reaction back to mission control in Houston, "It was beautiful, just like our drills." On a later moon expedition, Apollo Captain Conrad, commented, "It's just like old home week. I feel like I've been here many times before. After all, we've been rehearsing this moment for the past four years."

SELF-IMAGE

YOU'VE GOT TO LEARN THE CORRECT SWING BEFORE YOU PLAY THE INNER GAME IN ANYTHING

There have been many self-help books written about the ability of this marvelous self-image to create new roles and new ways to grow. Every week there is a new book on the art of visualization for success. We are encouraged to think positively, to cut out magazine pictures of the house that we want, to see the stacks of one-hundred dollar bills in our briefcase, to smell the salt air and watch the sail furl on our new sailboat, to imagine ourselves confident, attractive, and successful. We are told that all we have to do is see ourselves standing in the winner's circle with the Gold Medal around our necks and the National Anthem playing, and we're on our way to the Olympics.

Yet, most of us, no matter how hard we try, no matter how hard we visualize, go back to being ourselves. There is a Winner's Edge that separates the fictitious winners from the real winners. There is a true attitudinal skill that helps us utilize this self-image to make real accomplishments instead of pipe dreams. In order to be a tennis star, it is not enough to play the inner game of tennis, to let your mind flow free, and to let your creative subconscious play for you. While it is true that tennis stars visualize where the next shot will be placed a few microseconds before their rackets make contact with the ball, they have been relentless, persistent practitioneers year after year. I remember as a young boy, as caddy at La Jolla Country Club, I used to caddy for a businessman named Fred Littler, who had a young son, Gene, who was a couple of years ahead of me in high school. Day after day, week after week, year after year, I remember shagging golf balls, standing out at the 75-yard, 100-yard, 150-yard marker while Gene Littler would hit hundreds of practice shots into my leather bag as I stood at each marker. It is true that Gene Littler was developing the self-image of the good golfer. It is true that he had high self-esteem. It is also true that he had tremendous awareness of his potential and how exciting it would be to be a winner on the Professional Golfers' Association (PGA) tour. But I believe that more than any other characteristic the ability for Gene Littler to repeatedly practice on the actual golf tee, learning the correct golf swing and execution of a golf shot, observing other highly successful professionals, and then practicing winning, rather than losing, was the key to his success. When Gene Littler would hit a bad shot upon occasion, I believe that his thought was: "Get it toward the pin; you can do it better. Try it again, you'll do it better next time." When he would hit a shot right straight to the pin, I also believe that his confirming self-image self-talk was: "That's more like me; keep it there."

YOUR SELF-TALK CONFIRMS OR DENIES YOUR SELF-IMAGE

Some years ago, *Reader's Digest* told of a class of high-school basketball players with similar skills, who were divided into three separate groups to conduct an experiment. Group One was told not to practice shooting free throws for one month. Group Two was told to practice shooting free throws in the gym every afternoon for an hour for a month.

SELF-IMAGE

Group Three was told to practice shooting free throws in their imaginations every afternoon for one hour for one month. Group One slipped slightly in their percentage free-throw average; Group Two increased about two percentage points; and Group Three increased two percentage points. Ridiculous! How could your free-throw average improve as much from practicing in your imagination as from actual practice in the gym? Simply because in your imagination you never miss, unless you want to, or unless it's your habit.

When you practice in your imagination, you have the ability to picture another swisher and another. Therefore, your practice can make perfect. In the gym, when you make one or two in a row, your self-talk after the performance might be, "Gee, I sure hope I can continue," or "I hope I don't miss," or "That was a lucky one." In the gym, when you miss one or two, your self-talk might be, "Get it in, you klutz," or "There I go again." Just as important as your self-image before a contest or performance, your self-talk immediately after a performance usually conforms to your current self-image and confirms that you keep your aim locked near your present performance. I believe that the self-talk feedback immediately after every performance is just as important or more important than the simulations before the performance. It means just as much how we respond to our performances, whether good or bad, as how we anticipate them in advance. This is why some people are frustrated and fail, no matter how many self-help books they've read and no matter how much they think they understand the idea of imagining success. In the living room, when they are practicing skiing, they can get all the good feelings and see all the visualizations of success. However, once up on the slopes, coming straight down the ski run, which has been appropriately called "Adios," their imagination of success quickly turns into stark terror as they begin to lose control and consider the prospect of rolling down the hill or going into a tree. Falling on a ski slope is inevitable; however, it is the response to the fall and the immediate anticipation "That's not like you" or "I'm going to get back to being my good self," that accounts for a person's ability to overcome failure and to continue to see success. Just as we learned when we first rode our bicycles, it's a question of trial and error, and trial and error/success; trial/error/success; trial/-success; success/success/success.

THE SELF-IMAGE/PERFORMANCE/ SELF-TALK CYCLE

When a child of ten to twelve months old first considers the possibilities of walking, the child sees the adults walking and pictures the possibility of walking being a profitable experience. As the parents give him encouragement by holding out their arms or placing something interesting on top of a table just out of reach from a crawler, the child sees the possibility of walking as profitable. By experimenting, the child begins to take unsure, wobbly steps forward. Invariably, the first attempts at walking result in a substantial number of falls, a bump on the head, a near miss hit on the coffee table, a very hard landing on one's rear end, and certainly a frightening experience. However, not associating falling with failure, but only as a temporary inconvenience, the child's next thought is how to get up again and get the piece of candy on the table or get to the parent's beckoning arms.

I call this the self-image/performance/self-talk cycle. The self-image or the imagined goal determines the performance and the performance is usually consistent with the self-image that has been set in advance. However, many times in our lives our performance is either higher or lower than our goal or than our imagined ability. Therefore, it is our response to our performance in words, pictures, and emotions that just as much determines our self-image as does our imagined concept of ourselves before we ever attempt to perform in the first place.

THE BED-WETTING SYNDROME

Let me give you a good example. One of my sons wet his bed consistently for the first six and one-half years of his life. I don't know whether it was because he had early feelings of inadequacy because he was the youngest child, or because he received too little or too much attention. I only know that he consistently wet his bed every night like an automatic sprinkler. After he wet his bed, I usually confirmed his bed-wetting to him by reminding him what he was doing and chiding him that if he continued to wet his bed, I'd send him to the first grade with rubber pants on and certainly, "big boys don't wet their bed." This simple reminder after his performance confirmed that self-image that he had of himself as a bed-wetter, and he performed to confirm that image by wetting his bed even more, every night.

Not fully understanding how the self-image worked, I

105

decided to try to get directly onto my son's performance level and forget about any of that imagination stuff. I simply informed my wife that my son would get no more liquid after six P.M. I figured if I went directly to the source of the problem, then it would take care of itself. Somehow, even though he had no liquid with dinner, he managed to manufacture his own water and consistently continued to wet his bed. He knew who he was: He was a bed-wetter if he ever saw one. Not discouraged with these early frustrations in changing his performance, I proceeded to do what every good parent does when their child consistently wets his or her bed: I woke my son up at odd hours of the night, making sure to see if he was dry first, and then proceeded to try to make him perform as he should. When my wife and I would come home after an evening out, I would get my son up and make him stand in his pajamas, barefooted on the cold, tiled bathroom floor in front of the "john." What did I accomplish? I taught my son how to stand in his sleep, rocking back and forth on the cold, tiled bathroom floor in his pajamas for 15 to 30 minutes at a time. He never once used the bathroom facility, but waited until I put him back into bed and then proceeded to wet his bed as only he knew how to do.

One evening when I was in the living room reading a book, he walked into the living room, lifted up the cushion on the sofa and proceeded to go there. In addition to teaching him how to stand up in his sleep in the bathroom, I had also taught him how to walk in his sleep. But I had done nothing to break him of the habit of wetting his bed. In fact, now, I had even taught him how to wet the sofa as well.

IMAGINING A BEAUTIFUL, DRY TOMORROW—TONIGHT!

In order to change the performance, it is first necessary to change the self-image and the performance will follow. Finally accepting this fact, I proceeded to get into my son's self-image/performance/self-talk cycle to see if I could "dehypnotize" him out of being a bed-wetter by giving him new input and new self-talk as a nonbed-wetter.

The process was simple, and the results were amazing. Since this self-image is time grown, it is not possible to simply hypnotize someone and change him instantaneously into a nonbed-wetter. This is where self-talk simulation comes into play. Since we all talk to ourselves in words, pictures, and emotions at three to four hundred words a minute every single waking moment of our lives, the best method for modifying or changing the self-image is to engage in new simulated self-talk that literally suggests or creates a new self-image about that particular action or act. I tried the theory out.

The next evening I went into my son's room to tuck him in at bedtime. We sat quietly on his bed and had a pleasant conversation about the events of the day. I engaged him in a conversation, which I hadn't done in a long time with my six-year-old boy. As parents today, you and I spend less than 60 seconds alone with each child, one-on-one, when they are most receptive to input. This particular evening was the first night in many weeks when I had broken this general statistic. I looked at my

107

son and smiled and began to run my fingers through his hair and look into his eyes. I remember getting a lump in my throat as I looked at him and said, "You know, son, I really love you. You're really special. I'm really glad you're my son, and I'm very proud that I wear your name, too. I realize that I've been cross and angry with you a lot, but I just wanted you to know tonight how much I love you and how special you really are to me." I think I caught a surprised look of wonder in his eyes, which made the lump in my throat grow even larger. Perhaps it was hard for a bed-wetter to believe that he was so special in his father's eyes. I told my six-year-old son I'd like to play a little new game with him called "Words, Pictures, and Feelings." I asked him if he could close his eyes and see his own face with his eyes closed in his imagination. Different from many adults, it was easy for my son to close his eyes and see himself. I asked my son if he could see himself brushing his teeth with toothpaste. This was easy and he and I proceeded to brush our teeth in our imagination as we were sitting on his bed. I next proceeded to ask him to imagine himself walking on the beach with me that night. This was a fun game for him and he and I proceeded to take a walk by La Jolla Shores, from the Marine Room down to the Scripps Pier. As we walked along in our imaginations, squishing our toes in the wet sand and running as the waves came in to try to keep from getting wet, he advised me that I had gotten my pants legs wet from walking too close to the water. He also told me to be careful not to step in the seaweed as we walked along. We both enjoyed the walk together very much.

THE KEY TO BEHAVIOR
MODIFICATION

I then proceeded to give him what I believe to be the key to behavior modification and the effective utilization of simulated self-talk to modify the self-image. As we sat in a relaxed environment, during a time when he was most receptive to new information, just before bedtime (when his mind was nearly in neutral), I proceeded to describe the events of tomorrow to my six-year-old son. I told my son that he and I were together at six A.M., and it was tomorrow morning. We were in his bedroom, and as he opened his eyes at six A.M. the birds were singing, the sun was shining, and it was a beautiful Saturday morning. Just as he opened his eyes, I came knocking on his door and said, "Are you ready, son?" And he said, "Almost." He jumped out of bed, *warm and dry,* pulled his jeans on and ran out to join me at the car. We had two packed lunches ready, jumped in the car, drove down to the marina, and he and I went fishing and had a marvelous day aboard our boat. Now I hadn't taken my son fishing for two years because I'd been too busy. In his imagination, I created the synthetic experience of tomorrow morning. But this was strictly a simulation. It was just an imaginary sequence. After all, it was Friday evening, the sun wasn't shining, and the birds weren't singing. He was warm and dry, but he hadn't gone to bed yet! Nonetheless, my son was able to visualize tomorrow morning as if it were really happening. He must have lain there for twenty or thirty minutes, going over the sequence of coming attractions, in this case, a very desirable, very positive, and almost thrilling experience for him. Although I don't fully understand the mechanism, I do know that the self-talk simulation at a time when he was most relaxed, just before bedtime, with a sensory picture of the winning achievement as if it had already been accomplished, was his Winner's Edge for the night.

IT WORKS! (IF YOU DON'T LOOK BACK)

The next morning at six A.M., just like drill, I knocked on his door, he pulled on his jeans, he was warm and dry and we did, in fact, get in the car and have a wonderful day fishing. This is the self-talk simulation of a nonbed-wetter. It is the simulation of the dry bed that works.

I remember helping a resident nurse attempt to break her five-year-old daughter of bed-wetting. She did exactly as I had instructed. She spent time with her child in a receptive moment, feeding the child a simulated self-talk that would modify the self-image with a preview of a coming good attraction. A week or so later, I asked the nurse how the self-image program had worked. She replied, "Oh it worked for a couple of days, but after the third or fourth day she went right back to being herself." That confused me slightly, and I said, "Well, did it work for a few nights anyway?" And she said, "Oh, it worked fine for the first, second, and third nights." Questioning her further, I said, "Well, when she woke up dry, what was your immediate response or what was your feedback to her when she woke up dry?" The nurse said, "Well, I simply told her 'I'm sure glad you didn't wet your bed. I'm so proud of you because you didn't wet your bed last

110

night.' " Well, there was the key. Even though the performance was the desired one, even though it was the goal, the self-talk feedback after the performance reminded her of her previous condition. "I'm so proud you didn't wet your bed," which confirmed the old self-image that she had been a bedwetter and got her right back into the old habit that she had almost broken.

I think this idea of feedback and of confirming the desired results, while never recalling or looking back at the former undesirable condition, is the key to developing an attitude that will give you the Winner's Edge in life. This one factor is the reason why sometimes the "inner game of tennis," the "inner game of golf," the "inner game of skiing," the "inner game of bridge," and the "inner game of sexual performance" don't work. Even after a new self-image, as a result of affirmative self-talk, creates a new performance, the former loser usually brings himself or herself back down to where they think they belong by discounting, discrediting, or by just saying how lucky they were not to be doing the old thing again. In other words, they look back.

PERFORMANCE = VIVID IMAGINATION × REPETITION

The Winner's Edge in developing a creative self-image is understanding that the self-image is time grown, layer upon layer. It cannot be erased and cannot distinguish between what is real and what is vividly imagined. It responds best to new images that are presented to it in a relaxed environment, with specific words, pictures, and emotions as if the

111

new image were actually being performed with relentless persistence and repetition over a period of time. This is why Bruce Jenner, the great Olympic decathlon champion, credited the winning of his Gold Medal (in addition to his punishing physical-fitness program) to the fact that night after night, before he went to bed, he looked up at the photograph of his own face, which he had superimposed on the body of a former Russian Gold Medal decathlon champion, and vividly pictured himself taking his victory lap as the decathlon winner. And Steve Cauthen, the boy-wonder jockey, who is the youngest Triple Crown winner in history, recalls vividly that when he was nine years old he rode a bale of hay around the yard as if he were winning the Kentucky Derby, the Preakness, and the Belmont Stakes.

THE NEW SUPER-LEARNING

The most amazing breakthrough in discovering the incredible ability of the mind to store and retrieve data in large quantities and with near-perfect clarity has been the work by Dr. Georgi Lozanov, a leading psychiatrist in Sofia, Bulgaria.

Dr. Lozanov has developed a method of cue-reinforced learning, which we will be hearing about on a worldwide basis in the 1980's as "Suggestology" or "Suggestopeadic Learning." Originating in Bulgaria and monitored by the United Nations, this innovative program reteaches the broader areas of the mind and brain by combining the techniques of relaxation with the aid of soft music, psychology of suggestion, psychodrama, and repeated listening.

SELF-IMAGE

Dr. Lozanov's experiments with learning have stunned educators throughout the world. He enabled first-grade students to learn more than a thousand words of a foreign language in a single day! Plus, he is teaching first graders complicated algebraic equations and calculus derivatives so that they understand as well as learn the techniques of solving problems that would strain the minds of most high-school seniors and college sophomores. And these are just average first graders, six years old!

WHAT *THE DEER HUNTER* AND *COMING HOME* FORGOT TO MENTION

The more emotional and illustrative examples of the use of the imagination and simulation for the accomplishment of a desired goal have been recounted to us through the experiences of our prisoners of war returning from Vietnam.

As a volunteer rehabilitation coordinator, I had the first-hand experience of learning about some of the most remarkable mental accomplishments I've ever known. Did you hear or read in detail about the prisoners' habit patterns and practice sessions during their three to seven years of deprivation and boredom? What would you do if you were locked up, with no end in sight? Sleep? Read? Get depressed a lot? Feel sorry for yourself? Resent the folks back home? Go insane? Or would you, as many of them did, make prison a self-improvement, self-image retreat? Several of our POWs made guitars out of wooden sticks and strings. Although their crude instruments made no sound at all, those who knew how to play practiced from memory, listening in their imaginations. They taught each other many new chords, finger positions, and songs. Some who had never held a guitar before are now accomplished guitarists. Seven years is a long time! Other POWs at the Hanoi Hilton fashioned piano keyboards by taking a flat board and pencil and sketching the keys to their actual size. Although their "Steinways" were silent and unplayable, they practiced day after day songs like "Clair de Lune" and enjoyed their favorite selections. There were no Bibles at the Hanoi Hilton, so the POWs pooled their memory banks and reconstructed hundreds of the most significant passages for their Sunday worship service. They communicated via Morse code by tapping on pipes between their cells. They taught each other skills, from memory, discussed and rediscussed boyhood experiences of mutual interest and value, created complete mental diaries while in solitary confinement, invented hundreds of money-making ideas, and perhaps most importantly, gained perspective by remembering and sharing the great ideals that are the foundation of their country's greatness.

COLONEL GEORGE HALL: THE EPITOME OF WINNING SIMULATION

Perhaps the most dramatic story coming back from the Vietnam War is the true story of Air Force Colonel George Hall. While in solitary confinement, he played an imaginary round of golf each day for five and one-half years as a POW in North Vietnam. Like Steve McQueen in the movie, *Papillon,* Colonel George Hall paced back and forth in his cell in

SELF-IMAGE

order to keep sane and to keep from going crazy for five and one-half years. He practiced relentless self-discipline.

Colonel Hall recognized that we have two choices in life: either play back haunting memories of fears, creating neurotic ideas of death, disease, confinement, fear, and hopelessness or play back winning experiences from the past and previews of coming "Oscar-winning attractions." In his black pajamas and bare feet and in his solitary cube, Colonel Hall played a round of golf every day for five and one-half years. He put every Titlist 1 ball between the blue tees. He hit his drives, straight and true, down the middle of a plush green fairway, perhaps Pebble Beach or Augusta National. Every course he had ever played before, he replayed in his imagination every day for those five and one-half years. He replaced every divot, fixed every ball mark in the green, raked the sand trap again, chipped onto the green, pulled out the flag, got on one knee and checked the break to see whether it broke toward the ocean or up the hill, putted down the hole and walked on to the next tee, washing his ball in the ball wash of his imagination.

Those mental simulations paid off when he got back to the real thing. After seven years of not actually playing golf, after five and one-half years in solitary confinement, and less than one month after his release, he was back in form. Colonel Hall played in the New Orleans Open, paired with Orville Moody, the old pro. He shot a 76! Right on to his four-stroke handicap. The news media ran up after the round and said, "Wow, Colonel Hall, congratulations! That was really what you call beginners' re-entry luck, right?" Colonel Hall smiled and said, "Not really. I never three-putted a green in all my five and one-half years."

115

PRACTICING WITHIN, WHEN YOU'RE WITHOUT!

The Winner's Edge is practicing within when you're without. It's actually seeing yourself doing, within, when you are without. It is recalling and reliving those winning experiences from your past, to dwell on successes rather than failures. It is creating the synthetic experiences in the future, like the astronauts, by taking the correct theoretical information or data from other winners who have gone before you and practicing it as if you had accomplished it yourself before. Winning, then, is either recalling your own winning experiences or synthetically practicing those experiences you have yet to feel.

When winners are without, they work and practice to toughen themselves to the task. They know that the imagination is the greatest tool in the universe; It is the only universe for a prisoner of war. It is our creative universe for success.

ACTION REMINDERS FOR A CREATIVE SELF-IMAGE

Here are some action reminders to help you develop a creative self-image toward that critical attitude for success that makes up the Winner's Edge:

1. *Read a biography this month and each month.* The subject should be the life story of someone who has reached the top in your profession or in your major hobby, or just

someone you admire. As you read, imagine yourself as the person you are reading about.

2. *During the next thirty days, visit a military aviation flight simulator, an airline-pilot training simulator,* or a computer simulation or training facility at a university. Get current, first-hand experience with state-of-the-art simulation.

3. *Listen to audio-cassette tapes on the art of visualization and simulation.* Learn the steps for conditioning your own mind to relax and become more receptive to your own self-talk and suggestions. Record your own goals, in your own voice, on an audio cassette. Listen to music and play your cassette at the same time softly in the background. Concentrate on the music and let the voice cassette flow in unnoticed.

4. *Write a two-page resume of your professional and personal assets,* as if you were going to apply for the job of your lifetime. Instead of past experiences, list your maximum current potential and ultimate future growth potential. Read this two-page autobiography every week and revise it every two months. Show it only to those individuals whom you believe can and will help you toward your goals.

5. *Take stock this weekend of those images with which you display yourself.* Since the self-image is the visual, conceptual display of self-esteem (clothes, auto, home, garage, closet, dresser drawers, desk, photos, lawn, garden, etc.), make a priority list to get rid of all the clutter and sharpen up all the expressions of your life.

6. *Limit your television viewing to stimulating, special shows.* If you just watch television as a habit, tunnel

117

vision will set in and creative imagination will vanish. The same goes for your children!

7. *Set aside twenty to thirty minutes a day,* whether commuting to and from your place of business, at lunch, or in the morning or evening. As you relax during this time, imagine yourself achieving and enjoying your most personal desires. See them as if you were previewing three television shorts. Picture yourself in one sequence achieving a professional triumph (imagine the award ceremony, promotion announcement, or bonus payment). Picture yourself in another scene involving family happiness (imagine a special reunion or an outing together). Picture yourself in another setting in which you alone are relishing a personal victory (imagine a tennis or golf championship, or a weigh-in at the health club). Get the actual sensation of each event and how good it feels to experience each one. This canned role-playing is not just for salesmen and not just a seminar exercise on effective communication. It really works.

8. *Control your self-talk to elevate your best self-image* of a winning performance after every important performance in your life, whether it's closing a sale, speaking in front of a group, communicating with employees, playing a sport, or dealing with loved ones. If you performed well, your self-talk should be, "That's more like me." If you performed badly, your immediate self-talk should be, "That's not like me. I perform better than that." Then you should replay the action correctly in your imagination.

9. *Be relentless and persistent in your rehearsing of your goal achievements.* Both losing and winning are learned hab-

its. It takes days and weeks of constant practice to over-come old, entrenched attitudes and lifestyles.

10. *Go for a walk on the beach, in the country, or to the park and recall your childhood play.* Dust off and oil your imagination. It rules your world!

V
SELF-EXPECTANCY

SELF-EXPECTANCY is a self-fulfilling prophecy. It is the idea that what you fear or expect most will likely come to pass; the body manifests what the mind harbors. True self-expectancy is synonymous with commitment, purpose, faith, obsession, a burning desire. It is the single most outwardly identifiable trait demonstrated by a winning human being. Positive self-expectancy is pure and simple optimism, in the face of all odds. Self-expectancy is the key to motivation. It begins where the self-image leaves off. It takes the words, pictures, and emotions of imagination, and fuses them into energy and action by commitment. Winners have positive self-expectancy which creates desire. They are dissatisfied with the status quo. They want change for the better.

There never was a real winner in life who didn't want and expect to win. Scores of achieving people in every walk of life are all around us, yet few of us ever think of the long and arduous process that led them step by step to their goals.

121

Who, for instance, remembers that Winston Churchill was a poor student, or that Althea Gibson came from the back alleys of Harlem to the front court at Wimbledon, that Franklin Delano Roosevelt and Pancho Segura both had polio, that Beethoven was deaf, that Tom Dempsey kicked the longest field goal in NFL history with half-a-foot, that Margaret Thatcher, the prime minister of England, lived over her father's grocery store in England until she was 21. They all wanted something special for themselves, in spite of their early track record. In spite of their bloodlines or their home lives, they all had the desire to win; they wanted to win and they expected to win.

MOTIVATION IS AN INNER DRIVE

Many people have the mistaken idea that personal motivation is an option, like an hors d'oeuvre that can be taken or left alone. But everything an individual does, whether positive or negative, intentional or unintentional, is a result of motivation. Everyone is self-motivated, a little or a lot, positively or negatively. Even doing nothing is a motivation.

Motivation is a much maligned, over-franchised, over-promoted, and misunderstood term. The word motive is defined as that within the individual, rather than outside, which incites him or her to action; an idea, a need, a notion, or organic state that prompts an action. Motivation is a force which moves us to action, and it springs from inside the individual. Defined as a strong tendency toward or away from an object or situation, it can be learned and developed. It does not have to be inborn. For too long, however, it has been wrongly assumed that motivation is extraneous, that it can be pumped in from the outside through incentives, pep talks, contests, rallies, and sermons. Such activities do provide concepts, encouragement, awareness, and inspiration for individuals to turn on their creative powers (but only if they want to). And that's the secret. Lasting change is effected only when the need for change is both understood and internalized. Until the reward or incentive has been interpreted and internalized, it has no motivating power.

The real winners in life are people who have developed a strong positive self-expectancy. They have the ability to move in the direction of the goals or images they set, or roles they want to play, and will tolerate little distraction. In the face of discouragement, mistakes, and setbacks, this inner-drive or commitment keeps them moving upward toward self-fulfillment.

FEAR MOTIVATION: COMPULSION AND INHIBITION

Self-expectancy is an emotional state. The great physical and mental motivators in life—survival, hunger, thirst, revenge, love—are all charged with emotion. Two key emotions dominate human motivation with opposite, but equally dramatic results—fear and desire.

Fear is the most powerful negative expectancy and motivating force in the human system. It is the great compeller and the great inhibitor. Fear restricts, tightens, panics, forces, and ultimately scuttles plans and defeats goals. Fear vividly replays haunting experiences of failure, pain, disappointment, or unpleasantness and is a dogged reminder that the same experiences are likely to repeat themselves. The consuming prison words of the fearful person are likely to be: "I have to" (the compulsion); "I can't" (the inhibition); "I see risk"; and "I wish." Negative tension, induced by fear, creates distress, anxiety, sickness, and hostility. Carried to extremes, it can cause psychosis and death.

DESIRE MOTIVATION: GOOD STRESS!

Desire, conversely, is like a strong, positive magnet. It attracts, reaches, opens, directs, and encourages plans and achieves goals. Desire triggers memories of pleasure and success and excites the need to replay these and to create new winning experiences. The consuming words of the optimistic person are likely to be: "I want to; I can; I see opportunity; and I will." Desire is that emotional state between where you are and where you want to be. Desire is a magnetic, positive tension. Positive tension, produced by desire and expectancy, is like a bow pulled taut to propel the arrow to the bull's-eye.

Is tension or stress good or bad? It is good or bad, depending on whether you are optimistic or fearful. Stress is the response to any demand made on the body, and there is both good stress and bad stress. In a totally tension-free state, you are either comatose or dead. What individuals actually need is not a tensionless state, but the striving and struggling for a goal that is worthy of him or her. Mike Nichols, famous producer and Broadway actor, puts it this way, "Nerves provide me with energy. They work for me. It's when I don't have them, when I feel too at ease, that I get worried. When you get butterflies in your stomach before a performance, accept them as butterflies. Butterflies are nice. When they start to eat you, they are like moths. Moths in your stomach are not nice. They cause ulcers."

THE STRANGEST SECRET: AS I THINK, I AM

Rather than seek out all the new fad movements in an attempt to try to discover ourselves, we should get back to the basics in life and perhaps even refresh our memories that history's teachings have never changed. The best self-help book of all, of course, the Bible, says it all.

The one maxim coming from the Bible that has been passed on through the centuries that has never changed in meaning is the one that is indelibly etched in my mind as the greatest of all winning and attitudinal statements: "As he thinketh in his heart, so is he!" All of the self-help books from Dale Carnegie to Napoleon Hill to Maxwell Maltz to Wayne Dyer, spring from this one proverb, "As he thinketh in his heart, so is he." "As I think, I am."

The great Earl Nightingale, one of our most respected broadcasters and motivators in America through the years, interpreted this maxim, put it on record, and has the all-time, best-selling narrative phonograph record that has sold several million copies all over the world. Many businessmen and salesmen through the years have been motivated by Earl Nightingale's record of "The Strangest Secret." And "The Strangest Secret" in motivation is the fact that we, *literally, become what we think about most of the time.* This declaration touches all of us without discrimination. The promise is the same for the inquisitive youth, the ambitious man or woman, the nurturing mother, whether Oriental or Occidental, Black or White, Chicano or Indian, Islamic, or Christian. As you see yourself in the heart of your thought, in your mind's eye, so you do become.

YOU CAN'T MOVE AWAY FROM WHAT YOU DON'T WANT

Since we always move in the direction of our currently dominant thoughts, those thoughts that we are thinking of most, it is imperative to concentrate our thoughts on the condition we want and expect to achieve rather than try to move away from what we fear or don't want. Simply stated, winners focus on concepts of solutions, rather than on concepts of problems. The mind cannot concentrate on the reverse of an idea.

An excellent illustration of this is a true story concerning one of the most exciting World Series baseball games of the 1950's between the New York Yankees and the Milwaukee Braves. Warren Spahn, the great Milwaukee Hall-of-Famer, was on the mound for the Braves. Elston Howard, the power-hitting catcher for the Yankees, was batting at the plate. It was the classic confrontation: late innings, pitchers' duel, man on base, the deciding game of the series. The tension was paramount. The Milwaukee manager trotted out to the mound for a quick motivation conference with Warren Spahn. "Don't give Howard a high, outside pitch; he'll knock it out of the park!" were the final words as the manager finished the powwow. Warren Spahn tried not to throw the ball high and outside. He tried to relax and aim low at the inside corner. Too late! Like a neon light, the motivating image "high outside," was the dominant signal. It was a home-run pitch. Because of that one dominant thought, Milwaukee almost lost the World Series. Eddie Matthews came in with a home run to save the game for the Braves. But Warren Spahn to this day says, "Why would anyone ever try to motivate anyone on the reverse of what they want." And so it is with all of life's daily confrontations. You tell your children, "Clean up your room, you little pigs." And what do you get? You're right, a pigsty, and the kids say, "Oink, oink." Remind them enough and they know who they are. Winners know that their actions will be controlled by their current obsessions. Losers generally expect such occurrences as the loss of a job, bankruptcy, a dull evening, bad service, and failure. Most importantly, losers expect to feel bad and get sick, and do.

PSYCHE (MIND) TELLS SOMA (BODY) WHAT TO DO

Recent studies of the life histories of thousands of widely differing people have persuaded competent scientists that the probability of health changes, sickness, accident, even pregnancy, can be predicted. This finding is one of the many results of current research in psychosomatic medicine, the study of the relationship between the mind and the body and how each affects the other.

Scientists are now learning that disease is not necessarily

caused by germs. All persons have germs, but only a few become ill. Instead, the cause of disease is closely linked with the way individuals react to life. The link between stressful life changes, expectant anxiety and health changes seems to be associated with the body's immunity system, which makes antibodies to fight foreign material and germs. Situations which arouse fear and anxiety also suppress many body functions and they may suppress antibody production as well. Distressful situations may also upset production of hormones, which have a role in emotional balance. An emotionally upset individual is much more prone to accidents.

It is a fact that ulcers are not the result of what we eat, but what's eating us! Arthritis and bursitis are often associated with rigid and mentally restrictive individuals. "Montezuma's revenge" is not always the amoebas in the water in a foreign country, it is just as likely to be the expectancy. Seasickness is not just the imbalance in the inner ear, it is also passed on from parents to children as a hang-up that runs in the family. Asthma is much more pronounced and lingering in a child that has been dwelled upon and overly protected by a doting parent, one who is the victim of "smother love." An excellent treatment for this kind of asthma is a "parentectomy," at the Children's Asthmatic Hospital in Denver. Remove the parent from the child and the child begins to breathe more easily again.

VOODOO IS BELIEF, NOT WITCHCRAFT!

One of the leading authorities in the world today on the self-expectancy relationship between mind and body is Dr.

SELF-EXPECTANCY

Herbert Benson, associate professor of medicine at the Harvard Medical School and director of the division of behavioral medicine at Boston's Beth Israel Hospital. He is the author of the best-selling book, *The Relaxation Response,* and his more recent work, *The Mind/Body Effect,* documents the emotional relationship to many diseases.

In *The Mind/Body Effect,* Benson brilliantly explains the close interrelation between your mind and body in which thought processes lead both to disease and to good health. The concept of "voodoo death" is the extreme example of the potential negative effects of the mind on the body. Voodoo, as we have come to understand it, is a set of religious practices said to have originated in Africa as a form of ancestor worship. Among Australian aboriginal tribes, witch doctors practice the custom of "pointing the bone," whereby a magic spell is cast into the spirit of the victim. The purpose of such spells was to disturb the spirit of the victim so that disease and death would ensue. The many instances of such death were dependent both upon the victim's awareness of the spell cast and the victim's strong adherence to his society's belief systems.

One documented example in Dr. Benson's book tells of a young aborigine who, during a journey, slept at an older friend's home. For breakfast, the friend had prepared a meal consisting of wild hen, a food which the young were strictly prohibited from eating. The young man demanded to know whether the meal consisted of wild hen and the host responded, "No." The young man then ate the meal and departed. Several years later, when the two friends met again, the older man asked his friend whether he would eat a wild hen. The young man said he would not since he had been solemnly ordered not to do so by his elder tribesmen. The older man laughed and told him how he had been previously tricked into eating this forbidden food. The young man became extremely frightened and started to tremble. Within twenty-four hours he was dead!

In the Western world, many equivalents to "voodoo death" have been discovered in case histories. "You will die," the fortune teller predicted, "when you are forty-three." That prediction was made thirty-eight years before, when the fortune teller's client was five years old. The little girl grew up with the awesome prediction on her mind and died one week after her forty-third birthday, said a report in the *British Medical Journal.* "We wonder if the severe emotional tensions of this patient superimposed on the physiological stress of surgery had any bearing upon her death," the doctor said. They suggested she may have been frightened to death and said the case was that of an apparently healthy woman, a mother of five, who underwent a relatively minor operation. Two days later she was dead. The doctor said that the night before the woman confessed to her sister (who knew of the fortune telling incident) that she did not expect to awaken from the anesthesia. On the morning of the operation, the woman told a nurse she was certain she was going to die, but her fears were unknown to the doctors. An hour after the operation she collapsed and lost consciousness. A postmortem examination revealed extensive internal bleeding for which there was no reasonable explanation. A spokesman for the British Medical Association said, "There is no medical explanation to account for this. It seems rather like the case of the natives who die at the date and on the time the witch doctor predicts."

Consider, also, the death of Elvis Presley, the rock-star

legend. He died shortly before his forty-third birthday, of the same cause, at the same age, as did his mother. Although there has been much discussion as to the effect of the drugs that were involved, one of the least mentioned, more interesting aspects of Elvis Presley's death is that he may have been obsessed with it during the last year of his life and he probably expected it to happen!

FORTUNE IS A SELF-FULFILLING PROPHECY

What does all this have to do with self-expectancy and winning attitudes? Simply this, mental obsessions have physical manifestations. You become that which you fear, you get what you suspect, you are that which you expect to be. The power of the self-fulfilling prophecy is one of the most amazing phenomena of human nature. The winner in life, believing in the self-fulfilling prophecy, keeps his or her momentum upward by expecting a better job, good health, financial gain, warm friendships, and success. The winner sees problems as opportunities to challenge ability and determination. The equal but opposite force, in the self-fulfilling prophecy, to voodoo is optimism.

Perhaps the greatest optimist I've ever met and come to know is the professional golfer, Lee Trevino. What a winner! I've had the good fortune of observing Lee Trevino and the other top-money winning golfers on the PGA tour when I put together the Andy Williams–San Diego Open as a benefit for the Salk Institute. There is something about Lee Trevino that impressed me and stood out among all the others. Trevino is already a golf legend like Palmer, Nicklaus, Player, and Watson. He is the second all-time leading money winner in golf and is always in contention for the top spot. There is something special about his game and the way he wins. Lee Trevino does not have the powerful body of Jack Nicklaus. He does not have a picture swing like Gene Littler or Tom Watson. He doesn't look that good on the surface. But he has a magnificent obsession: He expects to win. He exudes and gushes optimism. Trevino says, "I'll admit I'm a money golfer. Every time there's a big purse, I go for it." When a lady asked him for his autograph, he noticed her gold pen. "My favorite color, gold," he quipped. In one interview he said, "I won the Canadian Open and the U. S. Open. I'd like to go for the Big Three. I think I can win the British Open, too!" He did, sure enough! Several years ago Lee Trevino caught pneumonia and was not fully recovered when the U. S. Open began. His doctor warned, "Better not play, Lee, you might get worse." Trevino answered, "Might get better, might even win." He came in second. Some time ago, he was hit by lightning and had a long interruption in winning following back surgery. After he won the Canadian Open again, he said, "That's more like me; now we're getting back where we belong."

THE INCURABLE OPTIMISTS!

What is it about this stocky, scrambling, self-approving, smiling, happy Latin that makes him so special? Lee Trevino is an incurable optimist. Don't try to tell him he is anything but the best, he just doesn't know any better. He makes his daily work look like it was playing on a swing set or the jungle gyms when he was a kid. Maybe that's the secret, he hasn't grown up to take himself or life too seriously. He says, "You know they used to call me a poor Mexican, but now they think I'm a rich Spaniard!"

Lee Trevino reminds me a lot of Willie Stargel. Willie Stargel, of course, doesn't play golf, but he is about one of the most inspirational baseball players in the game. As the captain and head motivator of the world-champion Pittsburgh Pirates, Willie Stargel always has an encouraging word for the rest of the team. After the Pittsburgh Pirates won the World Series in 1979, I watched Willie Stargel being interviewed on a national television program. The commentator asked Stargel, "How is it that you approach everything you do with such enthusiasm, as if you were playing sandlot ball again?" Willie replied happily, "Well, life is a fantastic game and you gotta flow with it; you gotta be happy every day." The newscaster questioned him, "But isn't there a lot of tension and pressure in the World Series? Isn't it one of the really tough times, and isn't it really like no other tough pressure-filled job?" "Heck no," replied Willie. "It's just a lot of fun and we always go out there to have fun every day." He said, "Have you ever heard the umpire start a game by saying 'Work ball'? Of course not, they always say, 'Play ball,' and that's exactly what they mean." This kind of talk may seem like professional arrogance. I see it more as real confidence, brought about by the habit of enthusiasm, which is optimism in action.

JACK NICKLAUS' JAR IS FULL!

Winners seem to know naturally that their actions will be controlled by their current obsessions. That's why they seem to be so optimistic all the time. As much as any present-day superstar in sports and in business, Jack Nicklaus, the golfing legend, personifies the quality of positive self-expectancy, by focusing on his dominant desires as opposed to his fears. One veteran of the PGA Golf Tour recently remarked about Nicklaus, "Imagine the mind to be a quart jar. Jack Nicklaus makes sure the jar is always full of positive thoughts—intentions of hitting accurate, good shots. The rest of us tend to fill the jar at least halfway with negative thoughts. We're thinking what can go wrong with the shot, rather than what should go right."

Nicklaus' mind is so permeated with the task at hand, there is no room for negatives. He controls every move to a specific end under conditions where most of our minds would be going a hundred ways at once. This tremendous ability to focus and concentrate on a dominant thought—on the winning action—is the mark of a winning superstar in every walk of life. Jack Nicklaus has applied this action quality to his many successful business enterprises. He has proven that when one concentrates on doing one thing extremely well, it will take seed and grow and multiply into many diversified opportunities.

LUCK IS THE INTERSECTION OF PREPARATION AND OPPORTUNITY

Winners see risk as opportunity. They see the rewards of success in advance. They do not fear the penalties of failure. The winning individual knows that bad luck is attracted by negative thinking and that an attitude of optimistic expectancy is the surest way to create an upward cycle and to attract the best of luck most of the time. Winners know that so-called luck is the intersection of preparation and opportunity. If an individual is not prepared, he or she simply does not see or take advantage of a situation. Opportunities are always around, but only those who are prepared utilize them effectively. Winners seem to be lucky because their positive self-expectancy enables them to be better prepared for their opportunities.

When asked by a news reporter how she thought she would do in one of her early career swimming meets in the United States several years ago, 14-year-old Australian Shane Gould replied, "I have a feeling there will be a world's record today." She went on to set two world's records in the one-hundred- and two-hundred-meter free-style events. When asked how she thought she would fare in the more testing, grueling, four-hundred-meter event, Shane replied with a smile, "I get stronger every race, and besides . . . my parents said they'd take me to see your Disneyland if I win, and we're leaving tomorrow!" She went to Disneyland with three world's records. At 16 she held five world's records and became one of the greatest swimmers of all time. She learned early about the power of self-expectancy.

INCURABLE OPTIMISM IS INFECTIOUS

Since all individuals are responsible for their own actions and cause most of their own effects, optimism is a choice. Achieving individuals—winners—are self-made, since their positive expectations make them what they are.

Positive self-expectancy is just as important in the home as it is for athletes on the field, salesmen on the showroom floor, and secretaries in the office. The enthusiasm of optimistic parents is contagious in the home. In their presence it is difficult to remain neutral or indifferent. Their gentle good humor and ability to look on the bright side of life establishes an *esprit de corps* among the inner circle of loved ones. Children become infected by this wonderful penetrating outlook.

One of my best friends, Zig Ziglar, is probably the top sales motivator in the United States today. And Zig defines his optimism in a way that always makes me smile. Zig Ziglar told me, "I'm the kind of optimist who'd go after Moby Dick, in a rowboat, and take the tartar sauce along with me!"

I remember watching an interview with Maurice Chevalier, the debonair boulevardier, America's number one Frenchman, with his jaunty straw hat, his crooning voice and his whimsical smile who made "Thank Heaven for Little Girls" a song we'll never forget. He danced and sang his way into the hearts of millions of people for over eighty years and on his eighty-second birthday, he was asked, "How does it feel to be eighty-two years old, Maurice?" The smiling Frenchman cocked his head and said, "When I think of the alternative, fantastic!"

HERE TAKE MY MONEY!

I know I'm a sucker for an optimist. When I see an optimistic salesperson, I say, "Here, take my money for your product." When I see an optimistic stockbroker, I say, "Here, take my money for your investment." To an optimist I'll always say, "Here, stand on my shoulders and see the view; how does it look up there?"

When I go into a clothing store and the optimistic sales-clerk says, "That suit just jumps to life on your body," I'm putty in their hands. Something happens to me when I look in the mirror and they say, "Boy, you really do something for that suit. It looks like a million dollars on you." With them so optimistic about me and the way I look, there is no way I'm going to leave that poor, forlorn, $350 suit hanging on the rack to die when it can come to life on my body. Of course I buy it!

I'll never forget when I went to get a spare tire at a Fire-stone Store and happened to walk into a Lincoln–Mercury dealership just to kill some time. I was met by a less-than-optimistic young salesman. "Wanna buy a car?" he asked. "Nope," I replied. "Just looking". "Figures," he said. "Things are going slow with the energy crisis and inflation." I said, "These new Continentals look a little smaller and don't seem to have as much razzmatazz in them anymore." "Well, we have to cut down on weight in order to meet the government's fuel economy guidelines," he complained. I said, "What kind of year are you having?" He replied, "Things are going a little slow." I said, "Any of these cars on the showroom floor for sale?" He said, "Of course, they're all for sale. Are you sure you don't want to buy one?" "Nope," I replied, "I'm just a literature hound." And I walked out.

Being a very curious individual, I decided to go down the Interstate to the other Lincoln–Mercury dealership I knew in San Diego. I walked on the showroom floor, only this time, unfortunately for me, I was met by an eternal optimist. This young man met me head on with a flashing smile, eyes fixed directly on mine, an outstretched hand, "Hi, my name's Stan Smith; what's yours?" He caught me a little off-guard, and I stammered, "Ah, my name's Denis Waitley." He beamed and said, "Hi, Denis!" I said, "You can call me Denis if you want to." He said, "You look like a Continental man to me." I said, "No, I'm just looking, I really should be down the street getting a spare tire at Firestone, but I just walked in to take a look around." He replied with a wink, "Oh, you wouldn't waste your time just looking around, not a man like you. You're here to buy, I can tell." Unnerved a little, I decided to catch him off guard. "What kind of year are you having?" I said, "Things a little tough?" He said, "I'm having my most fantastic year; this is my best year ever." I was quick to reply, "It's only January." But he came back with, "Well, it's my first year in the car business." I said, "Any of these cars for sale on the showroom floor?" He said, "They're all sold, sir; we put them on the showroom floor, polish them up, and send them out the door." He said, "Yours is on the back lot." He said, "Do you like the silver one, with the black top? Or do you like the all black?" I said, "You're not going to get me with those alternate sales-closing techniques," I said. "Of course, I'm not buying. But if I were buying, I'd buy the silver with the black top." He said "Do you like the leather or the velour upholstery?" I said, "I'm just looking, but if I were going to get one, I'd get the silver, with the black top, the leather upholstery, and the digital clock." I re-

138

minded him again I was just looking and he compli-
mented me on coming in at such an opportune time because this was going to be his first sale of the night. He
said, "You'll be glad you bought from me, because I'll
give you the best service you've ever had. Whenever you
want to come in and bring your car for service, which
will be very seldom because it'll run like a dream, I'll get
you in at 7:30 in the morning and get you right out. I
know how busy a man like you is. How would you like
to pay for it? Would you like to give me a small down
payment, or a check, or one of your business cards and
. . . you can take it with you if you want." Weakening,
but not giving in, I came back with my last and final ob-
jection. I said, "Well, I can't buy tonight. A purchase of
a Continental that substantial would require at least a call
or check with my wife, because I usually like to include
her on purchases this size." He came back, smiled, and
said, "Oh, I thought you were the kind of man that
didn't have to check with your wife for every little
thing." My eyes narrowed and I replied coldly, "I don't
have to check with her for anything." When I got home
that night, I told my wife the story of how I'd met another one of those incurable optimists and she exclaimed,
"Oh no, I hope you got the new spare tire that you went
down to Firestone for!" I retorted proudly, "Yeah, I have
got four tires parked right out front. Wait until you see
it; it's a dream!"

It's the amazing and sometimes painful truth that people
shy away from negative, pessimistic, unbelieving losers. They
gravitate to positive, self-assured optimistic winners. Optimism is like a forest fire: you can smell it for miles before you

see it burning. Optimism is like flypaper: you can't help getting stuck to it.

ENDORPHINS CREATE A NATURAL HIGH FOR OPTIMISTS

More than positive thinking, "How to Win Friends and Influence People," the deep hypnotic power within you, "Pollyanna," "Everything Is Beautiful, Baby,' and fundamental to the practice of Religious Science, recent discoveries about the brain have gripped both the public and scientific imagination and relate directly to this theory of why optimism is one of the single-most important traits in a winning human being. These discoveries are in processes in the body that produce morphinelike substances naturally. In other words, God created substances that operate on specific receptor sites in the brain and spinal cord.

These naturally produced substances appear to reduce the experience of pain and also cause the organism to feel better. The discovery of these internal opiates, endorphins, secreted and used by the brain, may be the beginning of a breakthrough to understanding joy and depression. Optimists may feel better about themselves simply because of endorphine that they have created by their optimistic thoughts. Presumably, these natural substances help people screen out unpleasant stimuli. Since the beginning of time, man has created his own external stimuli for optimism. Opium has been widely used, at least since classical Greek days and probably before. Other substances such as alcohol, cocaine, and more recently synthesized artificial substances such as morphine and LSD have had effects on the experience of large numbers of people.

OPTIMISM IS THE BIOLOGY OF HOPE

In his book, *Optimism: The Biology of Hope,* Dr. Lionel Tiger makes a strong case for the possibility that there is a location in the brain for creating good feelings about the present and the future.

Dr. Tiger suggests that we have developed this capability in our internal pharmacy ever since prehistoric times, when, as hunters, we optimistically entertained the idea of the successful hunt. He suggests that perhaps people who are pessimistic or depressed may look to external means to try to cure their depression with a variety of weapons: blood tonics, huge doses of vitamins, alcohol, sessions with psychiatrists and interior decorators, vacations, marijuana, Valium, cocaine, shopping sprees, and movies. I tend to agree with Dr. Tiger that optimism is the natural biology of hope. I'm equally excited about the discovery of the natural, internal opiates, which appear to be stronger than any morphine-based or man-made substance.

Evidence is building up that optimistic self-expectancy creates a natural high to help winners withstand pain, overcome depression, turn stress into energy, and persist. It has even been proven that women who have gone into labor, during the process of childbirth, secrete these marvelous natural opiates called endorphins to help them get through a painful process toward a desirable event, such as giving birth to their baby. Since it appears to be the natural thing to do, why not expect yourself to win in life?

Don't listen to the pessimists. Misery loves company. When they frown and ask you about inflation, tell them your goal is to conserve more, spend less, and earn more! Remind them that the value of your home is doubling every seven to nine years. When they gripe about the world situation and ask for your opinion, tell them you're working harder to set a good example for your family, fellow workers, and neighbors. Tell them you're getting your personal world in order, so that you won't throw stones from a glass house. And when they ask you why you're always so darned enthusiastic about life, tell them you're on a new drug called endorphine, which keeps you high for the new decade. They'll ask you where they can buy it and if it's illegal. Tell them it flows naturally and freely from within to the optimists, as a primary ingredient for winning.

IS THAT ALL THERE IS . . . TO A FIRE?

My house burned down (a hillside home in La Jolla, California, with a beautiful ocean view) several years ago. When I drove into our cul-de-sac and saw the fire trucks, rotating beacons, hoses, and smoke, I immediately thought, "Too bad for my poor neighbor's house." You see, I'm a hopeless optimist! But it was my house. The flames were 70 feet high, brilliant against the Sunday twilight. I panicked for a moment, desperately taking inventory of the crowd gathered in the street for a glimpse of my family. "Thank God." There they were: my wife, children, dog, cat, goldfish, hamsters, and two turtles, Lightning and Streak. Safe! I breathed a sigh of relief and with everybody else watched it burn.

My banker was standing there next to me in his bathrobe and slippers. "Wow, what a spectacular fire," he whistled. "Look at the windows pop out." And as the windows blew out, like a chimney flue, the ocean wind created a draft that destroyed the house like kindling wood. "Look at that Mark IV blow up in the driveway!" He looked at me shaking his head, "Unbelievable, fantastic; I wonder whose it is, Denis?" "It's mine," I answered quietly. He reeled, "Oh, no. You poor wretch! What are you going to do?" I smiled and shrugged, "I'm going to find a place for us to sleep tonight and start thinking about toothbrushes, underwear, and some basics for school and work tomorrow." I called my realtor, while the remains were still smoldering, and told her the house didn't stand up under "environmental conditions." She was confused until she drove over.

My banker told me I didn't seem upset enough with the disaster. I told him I was excited that my family was unharmed. He said, "Outside of their safety, how can you appear so optimistic and nonchalant?" I told him it was because I had finally cleaned the garage. He chided, "So what?" I chuckled, "My tax returns were in there along with all my personal files, and I've just been notified of a pending IRS audit. And now, suddenly, I have amnesia!" He pressed on, "What else is good about the fire?" I replied, "Look at this beautiful, ocean-view lot!"

As it turned out, it was really not such a bad fire after all. It actually was a blessing in disguise. Although we lost all of our material possessions, the precious family unit was intact. It was an exhilarating realization that, while fortunes can go up in smoke, they are rebuildable and expendable. We rented a small, furnished home near the beach and in the cramped, inconvenient, closeness I got in touch with each member of my family again, one-on-one, during the ensuing months, as we regrouped, tightened the belt, and resolvedly set about the team effort of reconstruction.

Peggy Lee, a special friend, sent me her album, "Is That All There Is (To A Fire)!" Yes, when there's life, that's all there is to any fire or setback. It's a temporary inconvenience.

Positive self-expectancy, winning optimism, turns problems into opportunities. I've spent time recently with Dr. Norman Vincent Peale. Bless his heart, he's still going strong in his eighties as the American poet laureate of positive thinking. Dr. Peale winks his eye, pounds on the table, and begs, "Give me more problems, God. I've run out of problems to solve and grow on. What I need today are some more of those good, tough problems!"

WINNERS MAKE THE BEST

Art Linkletter is also on the platform circuit with me, and I love to reminisce with him about our respective boyhood experiences in San Diego, where we grew up. (He looks young enough to be my brother, but went to high school with my mother.) Art relates to audiences all over the country his personal encounter with the tragedy that he transformed into positive growth. During the past 40 years he has enjoyed a uniquely successful career in radio and television. His season after season of *People Are Funny, House Party,* and his special way of conducting interviews in which "kids say the darndest things," have put him in a class at the top, along with Arthur Godfrey, Steve Allen and Allen Funt.

Art was skiing in Colorado, in the sixties, when his world came crashing down on top of him. His beautiful, talented young daughter, Diane, had lost her life as a result of an LSD drug trip, in which she was an innocent victim. Art's reaction went from utter despair and grief, to outrage and anger. For several years he bitterly denounced the drug culture and pleasure seekers and struck out as a vigilante to tell his daughter's story.

Art Linkletter is one of the best interviewers in the world, because (and he admits this) he is one of the most effective "listeners" in the world. By listening to the needs of others, his radio and television shows have been classics in human interest and child psychology. Drawing upon this ability, Art listened to the problems and needs behind the drug movement. He stopped fighting against what *is wrong* with our society and began to rededicate himself to what *is right* for our society. His platform speaking and hundreds of media interviews took a new tone of hope and optimism on what self-esteem and a healthy America are all about.

Rather than dwell on what went wrong, Art concentrated on how to go right. During the past decade, Art Linkletter has reached new heights in his personal and professional life, and he has enriched the lives of hundreds of thousands of individuals of all ages with his books, audio tapes, and public appearances. His marvelous, positive rebound from a devastating personal tragedy is best summed up by his timeless proverb, which he quotes at each platform speech:

"Things turn out best for the people who make the best out of the way things turn out!" Art's current contribution is living proof that he, like every other winner I've ever observed, makes the best out of the way things turn out.

PROBLEMS INTO OPPORTUNITIES: OLYMPIC STYLE

I shared the platform last spring at an AT&T meeting in Nassau with Herb Brooks, the dynamic, unorthodox coach of our "Cinderella" 1980 Olympic Ice Hockey Team. Recounting the steps that led to their incredible performance against the Soviet Union, that won the U.S. a gold medal and captured the heart of our nation hungry for any morsel of international pride, Coach Brooks said the team's impossible success was due to the reversal of its major "problem" into its major "opportunity." The U.S. team admittedly was young and inexperienced. The average age of the team was 21 years of age versus approximately 28 years of age per man for the Soviet team. On any given day, it was no secret that the Soviets could have been an even match for any professional ice hockey team in the world. And what made matters worse for the Americans going into the Olympic finals for the Gold, was that the Russians had blown them off the ice in their previous meeting at Madison Square Garden just prior to the 1980 Winter Games at Lake Placid.

The Winner's Edge for the United States Olympic Ice Hockey Team at the 1980 Games was turning a supposed "infirmity" into "victory." Coach Brooks briefed the team before the history-making match with the Soviets in a classic winner's style:

"We may not have superior talent. But the Russians are overconfident. They expect this to be a repeat of the Madison Square Garden game. Everyone expects our youth to be our infirmity and our downfall. It will be just the opposite. Your youth will be the winning difference. You have the youth, which means speed, energy, aggressiveness, and the spirit. I expect you to take the offense and beat the Russians at their own game. Make this 60-minute period your moment of greatness. You deserve and will win the Gold Medal. I expect the best from you. It's your time in history."

The rest of the story is history.

SELF-EXPECTANCY ACTION REMINDERS

Here are some action reminders to help you develop more positive self-expectancy:

1. *Wake up happy.* Optimism and pessimism are learned behavioral attitudes. One of the best ways to develop positive self-expectancy is to start early in life or at least early on any given day. Wake up to music. Have breakfast with someone you like who is an optimist. Listen to a motivational tape on your way to work. Read educational and inspirational books and articles that give you a lift the first thing in the morning.

2. *Use positive self-talk from morning to bedtime.* "Its another good day for me." "Things usually work out my

way." "I expect a great year." "Next time I'll do better."
"We'll make it."

3. *Look at problems as opportunities.* Make a list of your
   most pressing problems, the ones that block your professional and personal fulfillment. Write a one or two sen-
   tence definition of each problem. Now rewrite the definition, only this time view it as an opportunity or exercise
   to challenge your creativity and ingenuity. View the solution to your problems as you would if you were advis-
   ing one of your best friends.

4. *Concentrate all your energy and intensity without distraction on the successful completion of your current, most
   important project.* Forget about the consequences of failure. Failure is only a temporary change in direction to
   set you straight for your next success. Remember, you
   usually get what you think of most. Finish what you
   start.

5. *Find something good in all of your personal relationships*
   and accentuate the blessings or lessons in even the most
   trying confrontations.

6. *Learn to stay relaxed and friendly* no matter how much
   tension you are under. Instead of participating in group
   griping, single out someone or something to praise. Instead of being unhealthfully critical, be constructively
   helpful. When tension or anxiety enter the room, thats
   your signal to breathe slowly and deeply, to lower the
   tone and pitch of your voice, to sit back and relax your
   muscles, and to respond calmly to problems with suggested solutions.

7. *Think and speak well of your health.* Teach yourself and
   your children to use positive self-talk about your health.

SELF-EXPECTANCY

Too much attention paid to minor health irritations means there is a value to being sick, like a personal version of workman's compensation, which, if habitual, can lead to a host of allergies, aches, and exaggerated reactions. Remember that much of what ails you is the way you think.

8. *Expect the best from others, too!* Two of the keys to leadership are encouragement and praise. Vocalize, on a daily basis, your optimism and positive expectancy about your associates and family members. It's contagious!

9. *This week seek and talk in person to someone who is currently doing what you want to do most and doing it well.* This applies to skiing, acting, singing, speaking, hanggliding, selling, earning, or even being a good spouse or parent. Find an expert, and get the facts. Make it a project of learning everything you can about winners in the field. Take a course in it, or get personal lessons. And generate excitement by mentally seeing yourself enjoying the rewards of success.

10. *The best way to remain optimistic is to associate with winners and optimists.* You can be realistic and optimistic at the same time by realistically examining the facts of a situation, while remaining optimistic about your ability to contribute to a solution or a constructive alternative.

VI
SELF-DIMENSION

THE real winners in the game of life have developed an attitude of self-dimension. They look beyond themselves for meaning in life and put it all together as a total person. What a rare human being—a whole, total person. Although a total person who has been fully actualized has never been born, it is important to gain perspective on ourselves in life and look at the big, full circle rather than putting all the pressure on one point. One of the finest definitions of complete happiness is the definition given by an anonymous Greek, who said, "Happiness is the exercise of one's vital abilities along lines of excellence in a life that affords them scope."

Fulfillment or success has been defined as the progressive realization of goals that are worthy of the individual. It seems that you are happy and successful in life if you are doing your thing, you know specifically what your thing is, and that which you are doing earns you the respect of other people, because what you are doing benefits other people as well as yourself.

One of the most fundamental and important aspects of perspective and self-dimension in developing the critical attitude for success called the Winner's Edge is in understanding the necessity for human purpose. The human system is teleological, or goal-seeking, by design. Given random thoughts, or fixed on unrealistic goals too far out of sight, the human system, like a homing torpedo, will wander aimlessly around its world until it wears itself out, or until it self-destructs. The real losers in life are people who let life happen to them. They wander aimlessly around, just getting through the day, trying to indulge themselves in some new fad or pleasure. Or they simply self-destruct because of their inability to cope with the changing environment and changing fortune.

No one has given more clarity to the human necessity for purpose than Dr. Viktor Frankl, currently lecturing worldwide and a visiting professor at the United States International University in San Diego, California. A psychiatrist in Vienna at the outbreak of World War II, Dr. Frankl was a prisoner in Nazi concentration camps for the duration of the war. Frankl arrived at his conclusions about "Man's Search for Meaning" (the title of his classic book on the subject), after experiencing three years of horror in such death camps as Auschwitz and Dachau. Observing himself and his comrades, stripped of literally everything—families, professions, possessions, clothing, health, and dignity—he gradually developed his concepts concerning human purpose. Narrowly escaping the gas chambers and death by brutality many times, Frankl studied the behavior of both captors and captives with a curious detachment and lived to put his observations in writing. We in America have been reminded of the impact of these human sufferings in timeless motion pictures and television dramatizations, such as "Holocaust."

SURVIVORS ARE ACCOUNTABLE TO LIFE

Perhaps more than any other authority on human behavior, Frankl brings us knowledge that is first hand and that springs from objective evaluations of destitute humans living with the daily probability of death. These experiences enabled him to make a sharp departure from the theories of Sigmund Freud.

For example, Freud taught that individuals differed in outlook and attitude while healthy, but that if humans were deprived of food, their behavior would become more and more uniform as they resorted to the level of their basic "animal-like" instincts. But, Frankl states, "In the concentration camps, we witnessed to the contrary; we saw how, faced with the identical situation, one man degenerated while another attained virtual saintliness."

He noticed that men and women were able to survive the trials of starvation and torture when they had a purpose for their existence. Those who had no reason for staying alive, died quickly and easily. The ones who lived through Auschwitz (about one in twenty) were almost without exception individuals who had made themselves accountable to life.

There was something they wanted to do or a loved one they wanted to see. In the death camps, inmates told Frankl that they no longer expected anything from life. He would point out to them that they had it backward: "Life was expecting something of them. Life asks of every individual a contribution, and it is up to that individual to discover what it should be."

PURPOSEFUL OR PURPOSELESS?

While I was a naval officer stationed in Washington, D.C., following the Korean War, I conducted a study on how the Chinese and North Koreans interrogated and separated our prisoners of war into two categories with very basic questioning. By asking general questions of our servicemen who had been captured during the Korean War, it was relatively easy to identify the leaders or purposeful individuals from the followers or purposeless individuals. The questions were simple:

- Where are you from?
- Do you have a girl back home?
- What are you fighting for?
- What are you going to do when you get back?
- Are you going to college?
- What kind of career would you like most?
- Who is your favorite baseball team?
- Who is your favorite football team?

The soldiers and airmen who gave specific answers or simply gave name, rank, serial number, and nothing more were classified as goal-oriented and potential leaders and troublemakers. These prisoners were put in stockades in a maximum-security camp and were subjected to various forms of intimidation and torture in an attempt to crack their will and make them more susceptible to new ideas.

Those who gave nonspecific answers, who were wishy-washy and couldn't really tell you much about what they were doing or what they wanted to do, were put in a minimum-security camp as ideal subjects for further interrogation and behavior modification (brainwashing). These minimum-security camps in Korea were very much like country clubs. There were no guard dogs, no towers with machine guns, no barb wire fences. They were very nice barracks, with cafeterias, recreation grounds, and, most important of all, study halls for the learning of new materials such as Communist propaganda.

The prisoners in the maximum-security camps were badly mistreated, beaten, and, upon occasion, starved. And yet, many prisoners in the maximum-security camps escaped, attempted escapes, and constantly schemed about ways to get back to friendly lands.

The American prisoners in the minimum-security country club atmosphere in North Korea were given superior food, shelter, clothing, and medical care. And yet, incredibly, the death and disease rates were three times higher in these minimum-security camps than in the maximum-security prison camps! Having nothing specific to go for or get back to, in this country club environment, several of our young servicemen, in their early twenties, pulled the covers up over their heads and died of no apparent cause.

IF YOU DON'T STAND FOR SOMETHING, YOU'LL FALL FOR ANYTHING!

Perhaps a more relevant situation regarding purposeless and purposeful individuals is in the study of the conversion of individuals into members of various cult movements throughout the world. My own investigations of the Jim Jones tragic movement in Jonestown, Guayana, have led me to believe that people without purpose, who are just trying to find themselves, and who are in some investigative or transitional phase in their lives, are most vulnerable to the intimidation and conversion tactics of various pseudo-religious and so-called cult organizations.

This is obvious in observing the methods utilized by such groups in our nation's major airports, as they sell their books, develop cash flow to sponsor their movement, and sell their ideas to passing commuters. Invariably, they single out young servicemen who have either been drafted or are serving a tour of duty, knowing that these people are in transition in their lives and may not have specific goals they are working on at the moment. The cults also single out students, particularly foreign students, who are easy marks for professionally-trained interrogators.

YOU GOTTA HAVE A DREAM

The response to the challenges of life—purpose—is the healing balm that enables each of us to face up to adversity and strife. Where there is life, there is hope. Where there are

156

hopes, there are dreams. Where there are vivid dreams repeated, they become goals. Goals become the action plans and game plans that winners dwell on in intricate detail, knowing that achievement is almost automatic when the goal becomes an innercommitment.

What kind of goals are you committed to? For many people, getting through the day is their goal and, as a result, they generate just enough energy and initiative to get through the day. Their goal is to watch television—soap operas by day, cops and robbers and situation comedies by night. Having no goals of their own, they sit in a semistupor night after night with tunnel vision and watch TV actors and actresses enjoying themselves earning money, pursuing their careers and their goals. Since we become what we think of most of the time, whatever we are thinking of now, we are unconsciously moving toward the achievement of that thought. For an alcoholic, this could be the next drink. For a drug addict, the next fix. For a surfer, the next wave. Divorce, bankruptcy, and illness are all goals spawned out of negative attitudes and habit patterns.

If your goal is to retire, you'd better think twice, because true retirement is lying horizontally in a box, with a lily in your hand. There have been recent studies conducted by the insurance industry concerning retired military officers and businessmen who are looking forward to retiring and just doing nothing after 30 years of hard work. Do you know that they live about six to seven years in retirement? Not much time to enjoy their pensions and just doing nothing!

We all have the potential and the opportunity for success

in our lives. It takes just as much effort and energy for a bad life as it does for a good life. And yet, millions of us lead unhappy, aimless lives, existing from day to day, year to year, confused, frustrated, in a prison of our own making. Losers are people who have never made the decision that could set them free. They have not decided what to do with their lives, even in a free society. They go to work to see what happens. And you know what happens? They spend all their time making someone else's goals come true.

HELPLESSLY ADRIFT, OR ON COURSE

Thomas Carlysle compared human beings with ships. About 95 percent can be compared to ships without rudders. Subject to every shift of wind and tide, they are helplessly adrift. While they fondly hope that one day they'll drift into a rich and successful port, they usually end up on the rocks or run aground.

But those five percent who win, who have taken the time and exercised the discipline to decide on a destination and chart a course, sail straight and far, reaching one port after another and accomplishing more in just a few years than the rest accomplish in a lifetime. Every sea captain knows his next port of call, and even though he cannot see his actual destination for fully 98 percent of his voyage, he knows what it is, where it is, and that barring an unforeseen catastrophe, he will surely reach it if he keeps doing certain things a certain way each day.

IF YOU FAIL TO PLAN, PLAN TO FAIL

Winners in life start with lifetime goals. What do I stand for? What would I defend to the end? What would I want people to say about me after I'm gone? If I had one year to live, would I do in that year what I'm going to do this year? Winners also know how important time-priority goals are: a five-year plan; a one-year program; a six-month campaign; a summer project.

Most of all, winners know that the most important time frames are the groups of minutes in every day. Most people waste most of their waking hours every day going through the motions, chatting idly, shuffling papers, putting off decisions, reacting, majoring in minors, and concentrating on trivia. They spend their time on low-priority, tension-relieving projects, rather than high-priority, goal-achieving activities. Since they have failed to plan, they are planning to fail by default.

WINNERS HAVE A SHOPPING LIST FOR LIFE

Most people spend more time planning a party, studying the newspaper, or making a Christmas list, than they do in planning their lives. Winners set their daily goals the afternoon or evening before. They list on paper in a priority sequence at least six major things to do tomorrow. When they start in the morning, they go down the list checking off the items they have accomplished, adding new ones and carrying over onto the next day's itinerary those they did not complete.

159

Can you imagine if you did your grocery shopping without a list? What if you just went down to the big supermarket to see what was going on, to sort of play it by ear and find yourself? You'd see all the packaged television-advertised displays, a potpourri of irresistible goodies and items. Count Chocula Cereal, new improved Twinkies, Moon Pies, Star Wars and Star Trek T-shirts, Superman decals, the new Mister Clean, White Tornadoes (with special foaming action), Bionic Puppy Chow, two-second microwave TV dinners, and Waterless Dishwasher Soap. You'd be overwhelmed with goals you didn't set, didn't need, and didn't really want. Here you went to the supermarket for lettuce, tomatoes, and the ingredients for a nice salad, but since you didn't write it down and didn't really have it defined, you came home with a bunch of junk food.

Since the mind is a specific biocomputer, it needs specific instructions and directions. The reason most people never reach their goals is that they don't define them, learn about them, or ever seriously consider them as believable or achievable. In other words, they never set them. Winners can tell you where they are going, what they plan to do along the way, and who will be sharing the adventure with them.

LOOK BEYOND YOURSELF FOR PURPOSE

The Winner's Edge in self-dimension is to have a worthy destination and look beyond yourself for meaning in life. The greatest example of self-dimension a winner can display is the quality of earning the love and respect of other human beings.

I said at the beginning of this book that winning does not mean standing victoriously over a fallen enemy. Self-dimension is extending a strong hand to one who is reaching or groping or is just trying to hang on. Winners create other winners without exploiting them. They know that true immortality for the human race is when a caring, sharing person helps even one other individual to live a better life. Losers say, "I'm only concerned with me today." A winner's self-talk is, "I live every moment, enjoying as much, relating as much, doing as much, and giving as much as I possibly can."

HISTORY'S BIGGEST LOSER: I, ME, MINE!

The television dramatization, *Holocaust,* reminded us of the struggle for survival of people with a purpose. It also recalled for us one of the most infamous, self-made men who nearly ruled the world by using self-expectancy to achieve his goals, but who became the biggest loser in recorded history: Adolf Hitler.

When Hitler was a paperhanger, he convinced a few loyal followers that he was destined to be the ruler of the Third Reich. He used a distorted self-image and relentless simulation of his goals. He exuded a fanatic self-confidence that he projected to the masses in Germany, through the microphone, with methodically calculated words that fanned the fires of hatred and self-expectancy in his people to the deep-down belief of ultimate conquest of the rest of the world. He won every battle at the expense of other human beings and lost the entire ball game in the end, becoming one of the greatest tragedies in modern history, along with millions of innocent men, women, and children.

Adolf Hitler was a pathetic example of a "do it for myself" philosophy. He actually had extremely low self-esteem. This low self-worth is prevalent in those who yell the loudest and try to focus attention on themselves in a desperate attempt to gain external worthiness to make up for internal neurosis and psychosis.

The losers in life, like Adolf Hitler, have the philosophy of "do it to others before they do it to you." They have the "I win and you lose" attitude. It always, in the end, becomes the "lose-lose" attitude. But winners practice the "double-win" attitude: "If I help you win, then I win."

WINNING BEGINS AT HOME

True self-dimension starts with the inner circle: the family. Is your family a winning team or a chicken outfit the kids can hardly wait to grow out of? Are your marriage and friend-ships precious? Or have you lost touch, except for holidays, anniversaries, reunions, and parties?

Winners get it together with their loved ones, their friends, and with the community in which they live. They also love their careers, but are not married to them. Winners vote and care about the government of their cities, states, and nations, and their effectiveness, fairness, and honesty. And that of other nations, too. They build their spheres of relationships with evenly distributed emphasis. Are you a financial success, with plenty of money to spend, but no time left for your kids? I used to think I owned my kids, and later on I thought that maybe I leased them, and now I realize, as they have grown and flown the nest, that I didn't even have a lease option on them. Losers try to buy love and trust, and they always fail. Do you have a winning hobby as an outside activity, but a losing, neglected family on the inside? I know a man who got the civic-leader-of-the-year award for his contribution to the local boy's club, while his kids were being put in a juvenile home for stealing car radios.

WINNERS COMMUNICATE BY LISTENING TO OTHERS' NEEDS

The greatest communication skill of all is in paying value to others. That means really listening to others, asking questions, drawing the other person out, asking for examples, asking them to put it in other words, and feeding back for clarity and understanding. This skill of paying value to others, or creating other winners, is called the "I'll make him glad he talked with me" attitude. This great idea is so simple, it's almost deceptive. We have to examine it carefully to understand how it works and why.

The "I'll make him glad he talked with me" attitude is one that can become a whole way of life. When a successful individual faces a member of his family, a potential friend, a prospect, or an adversary, or when he picks up the telephone, his attitude is service-oriented, not self-oriented. His concern is for the other person, not himself. When we have someone else's interest at heart, not just our own, the other person can sense it. He may not be able to put into words why he feels that way, but he does. On the other hand, people get an uneasy feeling when they talk with a person who has only his own interests in mind and not theirs. There is an excellent reason why we all get these feelings about these people. It's known as nonverbal communication. It's the old business of "what you are speaks so loudly, I can't hear what you are saying." And it's tremendously important to all of us.

People, whether they know it or not, telegraph their intentions and feelings. Whatever goes on in the inside shows on the outside. We receive most of these nonverbal communications below the conscious level of thinking. Our subconscious level of thinking evaluates them and serves them up to us as feelings based on past experience. When we adopt the "I'll make him glad he talked with me" attitude, the idea of helping the other person solve his problems, we have his interest at heart. Then the feelings he receives agree with what he hears us say and the climate is right for both of us to benefit. Everybody wins with this attitude.

Winners in business, personal relationships, and in marriage, take full responsibility for success in the communication process. In other words, they never meet you half-way or go fifty-fifty. As listeners, winners take 100 percent of the responsibility for hearing what you mean. As talkers, winners take 100 percent of the responsibility for being certain that you understand what they are saying. By giving examples, by asking you for feedback, by putting what they said in different words, they make it easy for you to gain the true intent of their communication and they make it their goal to understand yours.

SELF-DIMENSION

I LIKE ME BEST, WHEN I'M WITH YOU

Most importantly, in their relationships with other people, successful individuals in life project constructive, supportive ideas. They are neither cynical nor critical. They accept another viewpoint as being valid, even if it is diametrically opposed to their own beliefs. They say, "I appreciate and understand your position, however, I may feel differently and, if so, I would like to tell you why my position may be different from your own." When Will Rogers said, "I never met a man I didn't like," I'm sure he didn't mean he approved of all the traits and characteristics of every person he met. But he found something he could admire in everyone. We get back from people what we give them. If we want to be loved, we must first be lovable.

Think back to the people who have had the most influence on you. You'll likely find that they are people who really cared about you: your parents, a fine teacher, a business associate, a good friend—someone who was interested in you. The only people you will influence to any great degree will be the people you care about. When you are with people you care about, their interests, not yours, will be uppermost in your mind.

This is most evident in marriage and parenthood. But it is also true in every other area of our lives. It has been said that, "Marriage is not looking at each other, but looking in the same direction together." And this is just as applicable to other aspects of life as it is to marriage. It's not looking at each other, but looking in the same direction together. Our success in getting along with others and communicating effectively with them depends upon this same principle. It depends solely upon our ability to help other people solve their problems. This is winning self-dimension. You'll know you're a true winner in the game of life when you hear this statement often from others that you meet: "I like me best when I'm with you." If a person says to you, "I like me best when I'm with you," what they are saying is, when I'm in your company, you allow me to be all that I can be. Your support and encouragement make me like myself best when I'm with you.

SELF-DIMENSION IS SPIRITUAL DIMENSION

Self-dimension goes beyond relationships with other human beings. It applies very definitely to an individual's relationship with God and nature. Loving and respecting creation, winners realize that it's not nice to fool Mother Nature. Nature is innocent, abundant—but unforgiving. We have exploited her resources and she is responding like a mirror, reflecting our gluttony and plunder with dwindling resources, pollution, unclean air, unsafe water, toxic food, and cancerous by-products of technology. As we change our environment to suit our short-range ambitions, we risk the very survival of the human race.

Self-dimension is understanding the vulnerability of the life process and the delicate balance of ecology. It is well to reflect and remember, those who owned the earth for thousands of years and who are now in the Hall of Fame of the

SELF-DIMENSION

Extinct. We need to know that New York could become Tyrannosaurus Rex and Los Angeles the Mastadon unless we cherish the natural environment and put back into earth at least as much as we take out. We can take our cues from our friends, the animals. Someday when Sea World has long gone dry, and all the birds have flown, and all the fish are gone, or on our dinner table, and all the animals are rubberized or polyester foam, available exclusively on stage at Disneyworld—someday a group of wisemen will deduce and calculate that what befell the animals may well be human fate. Someday, if we're not careful, we may find in some museum, a glass display that lights up when you press the rail, complete with tape-recorded spiel, that tells in 30 seconds of the day when man, too, roamed the planet earth, with his beloved friends, the animals. Self-dimension is being in harmony with nature and with the divine order that shapes the entire universe. It is seeing the perfection and beauty manifested by God in nature and accepting the imperfection in man's attempt to reshape nature in his own image, to rationalize his ignorance of the wisdom and intelligence behind life and creation.

Winners are able to put their own being in dimension with other human beings who lived upon earth nearly one million years before and are open to the idea that other forms of life, possibly more advanced, may be present in the outer regions of infinity, beyond the Palomar telescope, Apollo, Discoverer, and the space-shuttle programs. Perhaps more than any other dimension in the critical attitude for success that makes up the Winner's Edge is the individual's ability to tap that tremendous abundance beyond ourselves, "the spiritual dimension" that is our own creation.

I said in the introduction that I hoped this would be the last self-help book you'll ever need. In truth, the Bible is the greatest source of self-management guidelines. It's little wonder that it is the all-time best-selling work, by which most positive-thinking books have been inspired.

TIME: A CLOSE ENCOUNTER OF THE FOURTH KIND

After the dimension of purpose, which makes life worth living, the dimension of our relationship with other human beings, and the dimension of our own lives with that of nature and our creation, there is a final dimension that I believe to be the final cutting surface of the Winner's Edge. This fourth dimension is *time*. Time is forever the ruler of each of our lives. When we were children, time stood still. It took forever for Christmas and summer vacation to arrive. A day in grammar school seemed like a week. Our senior year in high school moved at a turtle's pace. Our twenty-first birthday was always way out in the future. A Saturday at the beach lasted forever.

The critical attitude in understanding the passage of time is developed in what I call "a close encounter of the fourth kind," which is a life experience in which you come face to face with the dramatic reality that there are no time-outs, no substitutions, and no replays in the game of life. It's the sobering understanding that the clock is always running. Your encounter may be a near miss on the freeway, the loss of a friend or a loved one, a wartime experience, a lengthy illness, or a visit to the burn ward in the intensive care unit at your hospital. Your encounter may be as subtle as a high-school class reunion or the discovery in the attic of an old photograph of you and your family. It may be the chance meeting of an old friend. Your encounter may be an innocent glance in the bathroom mirror.

Winners learn from their close encounters and develop a cherished respect for the passing and value of time. Losers begin to fear the passage of time, chasing it, squandering it, and, most of all, trying to hide from it beneath a superficial cosmetic veil of pleasures, fads, cults, and indulgences. Successful individuals understand the mortality of their body and are able to age gracefully as a result. They tend their gardens, like sensitive horticulturists instead of one-shot profit planters. They do not necessarily accept death as the final gun in the game of life. They see it as a transition into another plane, and, although they may never come to fully comprehend its meaning while living, they do not fear its eventuality.

TAKE TIME TO LIVE

Take time to look—at the rosebuds opening each day. Take time to listen—there may be fewer robins next spring. Take time for children—too soon they fly like arrows from the bow. Take time to play—when children grow up, they get old. Take time for old people—they live for the next visit from a loved one. Take time for your family—it's the precious inner circle. Take time for nature—you can't put it on your master-charge card. Take time for animals—it's their world too. Take time to read—books are the fountain of wisdom, and they take you where you can't go in person. Take time to work— you can't enjoy the view unless you scale the mountain. Take time for your health—it's the precious gift you're given that you don't recognize and appreciate until you have it no longer. Take time for yourself—enjoy your own peace and solitude, knowing that you are an island in a common sea in life.

"SOMEDAY I'LL": THE FANTASY ISLAND WE NEVER REACH

The Winner's Edge is understanding time. Winners don't live their lives in the past, becoming senile. They learn from it, not repeating their mistakes, but savoring each memory that brought them happiness. Winners don't live their lives in the distant future, safely out of sight, in that wonderful world called, "someday I'll."

One of the problems shared most frequently by unhappy people is that they allow their lives to be governed by what may happen tomorrow. They are always waiting for some incident to come about in the future to make them happy, when: they get married; the mortgage is paid off; the children complete their education; they make more money; they get a new car; the energy crisis is over; inflation is back down to a single digit; they complete some task, pay some bill, or overcome some difficulty. They are continually let down and frustrated. If the art of being happy is not experienced and related to the present time, it will not be experienced at all. You cannot base happiness on an uncertain event or possible occurrence. Another problem will always come along just as you find the answer to the previous one. Your whole life is a connecting succession of difficulties and problems, both large and small, which to the winners become no more than opportunities for challenge and growth. The only time for happiness is right now.

The "someday I'll" time never comes, but is safely procrastinated to the distant future. Procrastination is the fear of success. I used to think it was fear of failure, but now I know after years of study and costly experiences of my own that people procrastinate because they are afraid that they don't deserve the success that they know will result if they move ahead now. Because success is heavy, carries a responsibility with it, and requires an individual to continue to set an example, it is much easier to procrastinate and live on the "someday I'll" philosophy. Winners don't live their lives in the future, safely out of sight. They set goals in the specific, foreseeable future, which gives their everyday activities richness and purpose.

LIFE IS MADE UP OF SMALL PLEASURES CALLED MINUTES

The Winner's Edge is living in the present, in that only moment of time over which we have any control—now—and it's history—now—and it's gone. I would like to run Horace Mann's words in a classified ad in every newspaper in the world under lost and found: "Lost: one twenty-four-hour, twenty-four-carat golden day; each hour studded with sixty diamond minutes, each minute studded with sixty ruby seconds. But don't bother to look for it, it's gone forever. That wonderful golden day, I lost today." Life is not a race to come in first, but one to make last and best. True self-dimension is to live every minute as if it were your last, to always look for good, and to cherish the minutes and the lives that you encounter within it.

In a recent interview in *Parade* magazine, the great creative genius of current American television, Norman Lear, reflected upon his concepts of success and winning more sensitively than any other philosopher of modern times: "Throughout the American scene—television, sports, government—the message seems to be that life is made up of winners and losers. If you are not number one or in the top five, you have failed. There doesn't seem to be any reward for simply succeeding at the level of doing one's best. Success is how you collect your minutes. You spend millions of minutes to reach one triumph, one moment, then you spend maybe a thousand minutes enjoying it. If you are unhappy through those millions of minutes, what good are the thousand minutes of triumph? It doesn't equate. Life is made of small pleasures. Good eye contact over the breakfast table with your wife. A moment of touching with a friend. Happiness is made of those tiny successes. The big ones come too infrequently. If you don't have all of those zillions of tiny successes, the big ones don't mean anything. I don't know what my relationship to society is. Are people less bigoted than they were before "All in the Family?" But if there is one thing I want my children to learn from me, it is to take pleasure in life's daily small successes. It is the most important thing I've learned in fifty-seven years."

The true winners see their total person in such a fully-formed perspective that they literally become part of the big picture of life—and it of them. They have learned to know themselves intimately. They have learned to see themselves through the eyes of others. They have learned to feel one with nature and the universe. They have learned to be aware of time, their opportunity to learn from the past, plan for the near future, and live as fully as possible in the present.

I wrote two poems, one for women and one for men, that mean a great deal to me. I carry them with me wherever I go. When I am caught with too much idle time between planes at the Atlanta Airport, when I find myself looking out a hotel window at the blinking neon lights of some faceless city, when I'm in a hurry to get my credit card out so I can gas up and go, and the photos of my wife, kids, and parents fall out of my wallet on my lap; when I'm on a freeway, and just before I fall asleep at night, I recite these poems, silently to myself. They bring out the best in me and pull out some hidden resolve, energy, and dedication to make life more of a beautiful melody, in harmony with everything I touch. I hope you enjoy them and that they bring you a note or two of the dimension they give to me.

To the winning girl or woman of today, your positive self-dimension might be trying to say:

THE WINNER'S EDGE

MIRROR, MIRROR

Mirror, Mirror on my wall,
What's the meaning of it all?
Is there something more to life
Than to be a loving wife?

Yes, I'll love my children dearly,
But they'll grow up and come by yearly.

Dare I yearn for something more,
Than to cook and wax the floor?

What about the needs I feel,
Are my dreams considered real?

What about an education and
A voice to shape our nation?

Is my destined heritage
Just a two-fold color page
In some girlie magazine?
Just a sexy pin-up queen?

I've got a body and a soul,
I've got a mind, I've got a goal.

I want to learn, I want to teach.
I want to earn, I want to reach.

I want to fly from my cocoon and
Put my footsteps on the moon.

I'm not angry or rebelling, but there's
Something strong, compelling.

SELF-DIMENSION

I don't want to be a man,
I love the woman that I am.

I can give the world so much
With my special female touch.

Mirror, Mirror on my wall
Help me, help Him hear my call.
All I ever hope to be is
Free—to be that person, ME.

And for the winning male, at any age, here is my version
of positive self-dimension:

CRYSTAL BALL

Crystal ball, oh, crystal ball
Will my empire rise and fall
Like the Roman legions must
Ash to ash, dust to dust?

Is there something more to life
Than to build it for my wife
And to give our children more
Than their parents had before?

Go to work, earn the bread
Watch TV, go to bed
Sunrise, sunset, year to year
Before I know it, winter's here.

It's no scrimmage, no practice game
And there's no martyr's hall of fame

175

THE WINNER'S EDGE

Time, the speedster, takes its toll
And every day's my Superbowl.

Losers live in classic style
In the never-world of "Someday I'll"
They blame bad luck each time they lose
And hide with sickness, drugs, and booze.

Losing's a habit, so is winning
The way to change is by beginning
To live each day, as if my last
Not in the future, nor in the past.

To want it now, to dream it now
To plan it now, to do it now

To close my eyes and clearly see
That person I'd most like to be.

Crystal ball, oh, crystal ball
Help me hear my inner call
I think I can, I know I can
Become my greatest coach and fan.

And love myself, and give away
All the love I can today
I think I can, I know I can
Become a most uncommon man.

SELF-DIMENSION ACTION REMINDERS

Here are some action reminders for the development of that attitude of positive self-dimension.

1. *Ask yourself the question: "How do I fit* into my family, my company, my profession, my community, my nation, my world, and creation?"
2. *Pay value to your spouse or loved one today* with a touch and an "I love you." Flowers, poems, cards, and touches are evergreen!
3. *Tonight kiss a child good-night with an added, "You are special,* and I love you for who you are." And tomorrow listen to and play with that child as if you were a playmate again.
4. *Tell a parent or relative or friend* in person or by phone how much he or she means to you today.
5. *Make a contribution to something* or someone for which there is no direct payoff or obligation.
6. *This Saturday, do something you have wanted to do for years.* Something just for yourself. And repeat this process once each month.
7. *Treat people more like brothers and sisters.* And treat animals more like people. Treat nature more carefully and tenderly—she is precariously balancing our future survival.
8. *What are your lifetime goals?* What do you stand for, what do you want your children to tell their children about you? Jot down a one-page brief.
9. *What are your time-priority goals* in groups of years? For

177

the next five years, write one major goal in each of the eight following areas:

- Career
- Physical
- Family
- Personal Attitude
- Financial
- Public Service
- Educational
- Entertainment

10. Ask yourself the question: *"What am I going to do today, that is the best use of my time and that will directly benefit me and the others closest to me?"* When you plan your tomorrow, in the morning, either before you go to work or after you arrive, take a few minutes quietly alone. And then write your priorities down.

MAKE SOMEDAY BECOME NOW

Understand that you, yourself, are no more than the composite picture of all your thoughts and actions. In your relationships with others, remember the basic and critically important rule: "If you want to be loved, be lovable. If you want respect, set a respectable example!" As long as change is inevitable, why not play your hand to win? You can't change the heredity or the early environment you were dealt. But you certainly can change your *attitude* toward them and learn how to respond to life in a healthier, happier, and more worthwhile manner.

There are literally thousands of self-help programs and

books today, each with a different formula for self-actualization and individual happiness. The books each contain words of authors who were inspired to share their thoughts. You alone, the reader, give the message light. You turn the pages. You react, compare, recall, and respond. You close the book when you are through. Whether you put it back on the shelf or pass it along to someone who may enjoy it or need it, usually you continue your established ways and do little about incorporating some of the good points from the book into your own life. In other words, you go back to being yourself.

So here is one called "The Winner's Edge": How to develop that critical attitude for success. Now that you've read it, *go out and do it!*

BIBLIOGRAPHY

Allen, James. *As a Man Thinketh.* New York: Grosset & Dunlap, Inc., 1959; Lakemont, Ga.: CSA Press, new edition, 1975, softcover.

Benson, Herbert, M.D., *The Mind/Body Effect.* New York: Simon & Schuster, 1979, paperback.

Berne, Eric. *Beyond Games and Scripts: Selections from His Major Writings.* Edited by Claude Steiner and Carmen Kerr. New York: Grove Press, Inc., 1976; Grove Press, Inc., 1977, paperback.

———. *Games People Play: The Psychology of Human Relationships.* New York: Grove Press, Inc., 1964; Grove Press, Inc., 1964, paperback; Random House, Inc., Ballantine Books, Inc., 1976, paperback.

The Bible.

Briggs, Dorothy Corkille. *Your Child's Self-Esteem: The Key to His Life.* New York: Doubleday & Co., Inc., 1970; Doubleday & Co., Inc., Dolphin Books, 1975, paperback.

Bristol, Claude. *The Magic of Believing.* Englewood Cliffs, N.J.: Prentice-Hall, Inc., 1957; New York: Cornerstone Library, Inc., 1967, paperback.

Carnegie, Dale. *How to Win Friends and Influence People.* New York: Simon & Schuster, Inc., 1936; Pocket Books, Inc., 1977, paperback.

BIBLIOGRAPHY

Frankl, Viktor E. *Man's Search for Meaning.* Revised edition. Boston, Mass.: Beacon Press, Inc., 1963; New York: Pocket Books, Inc., 1975, paperback.

Fromm, Erich. *The Art of Loving.* New York: Harper & Row Publishers, Inc., Perennial Library, 1974, paperback.

Gardner, John W. *Excellence: Can We Be Equal and Excellent Too.* New York: Harper & Row Publishers, Inc., 1961; Harper & Row Publishers, Inc., Perennial Library, 1971, paperback.

————. *Self-Renewal: The Individual and the Innovative Society.* New York: Harper & Row Publishers, Inc., 1964; Harper & Row Publishers, Inc., Colophon Books, 1964, paperback; Harper & Row Publishers, Inc., Perennial Library, 1971, paperback.

Gibran, Kahlil. *The Prophet.* New York: Alfred A. Knopf, Inc., 1923.

Glasser, William, M.D. *Schools Without Failure.* New York: Harper & Row Publishers, Inc., 1969; Harper & Row Publishers, Inc., Perennial Library, 1975, paperback.

Harris, Thomas A., M.D. *I'm OK—You're OK: A Practical Guide to Transactional Analysis.* New York: Harper & Row Publishers, Inc., 1969; Avon Books, 1973, paperback.

Hill, Napoleon. *Think and Grow Rich.* New York: Hawthorne Books, Inc., 1966; Fawcett World Library, 1976, paperback.

Hoffer, Eric. *The True Believer.* New York: Harper & Row Publishers, Inc., 1951; Harper & Row Publishers, Inc., Perennial Library, 1966, paperback.

James, Muriel, and Jongeward, Dorothy. *Born to Win: Transactional Analysis with Gestalt Experiments.* Reading, Mass.: Addison-Wesley Publishing Co., Inc., 1971.

Lao Tzu. *Tao Te Ching.* Translated by D. C. Lau. New York: Penguin Books, Inc., 1964, paperback.

Lederer, William J., and Jackson, Don D. *The Mirages of Marriage.* New York: W. W. Norton & Company, Inc., 1968.

BIBLIOGRAPHY

Lindbergh, Anne Morrow. *Gift from the Sea.* New York: Pantheon Books, 1955; Random House, Inc., Vintage Trade Books, 1965, paperback.

Maltz, Maxwell, M.D. *Psycho-Cybernetics: The New Way to a Successful Life.* Englewood Cliffs, N.J.: Prentice-Hall, Inc., 1960; Pocket Books, Inc., paperback.

Lozanov, Georgi, M.D., *Suggestology and Outlines of Suggestopedy.* New York, Gordon and Breach Science Publishers Ltd., 1978, hardback.

Maslow, Abraham H. *The Farther Reaches of Human Nature.* New York: Viking Press, Inc., 1971.

Nightingale, Earl. *This Is Earl Nightingale.* New York: Doubleday & Co., Inc., 1969.

Osborn, Alex F. *Applied Imagination: Principles and Procedures of Creative Problem-Solving.* 3rd edition. New York: Charles Scribner's Sons, 1963, paperback.

Selye, Hans. *Stress Without Distress.* Philadelphia: J. B. Lippincott Co., 1974; New York: New American Library, Signet Books, 1975, paperback.

Tiger, Lionel, *Optimism: The Biology of Hope.* New York, Simon & Schuster, 1979, hardback.